gertrude's table

stories and recipes from my sicilian grandmother's kitchen

words and images   elizabeth periale

i corsi

Opposite: Gaetana Marta "Gertrude" D'Ippolito in communion dress, New York, c. 1906.

Opposite: New York World's Fair, Queens, New York, c.1939. L-R: Joseph Francis Periale, James Gabriel Periale, Paula Periale, Gertrude.

Opposite: Gertrude and Elizabeth Anne Periale, Spring Lake Heights, New Jersey, c. 1963.

Opposite, above: Frank D'Ippolito was a cook like his father, Don Peppino. Below: Frank admires a car . . . [see page 127 for detailed caption].

aperitivo

The aperitivo begins the meal and digestion. It stimulates the palate and can be an aperitif, like Campari with soda water, or small bites, like a dish of olives, nuts or cheese to nibble on while waiting for the next course.

Researching my family tree is a passion of mine, first fueled by a seventh grade civics class homework assignment. When I came home from school and mentioned my assignment at dinner one evening, my father, a newspaperman, suggested I interview his mother that weekend. I wrote down some questions to ask my grandma, Gertrude Periale, and he set me up with a microphone and tape recorder. Thankfully those precious tapes have survived—of my Sicilian grandma spinning tales of "Daddy's mother's uncle" and other colorful members of our Italian family.

That same weekend I also called my mother's mother and filled in the blanks from her side of the family. When I brought my family tree into class the next week and watched other students point to their grandmothers, grandfathers, aunts, cousins, etc. perfunctorily on their trees, I fidgeted in my seat in anticipation. Finally my turn came. I pinned my tree up on the wall at the back of the class and read off the names from my mother's side: Winship, Nichols, Averill. Then I switched to my father's side: Periale, D'Ippolito, Quartuccio, along with Grandma's stories—of Massimo the baker and Don Peppino the chef. My teacher and the class were fascinated. There were giggles on hearing names such as "Parin" Secundo Cerchio, and my grandma Gertrude, born Gaetana Marta D'Ippolito. Why were my relatives' names so funny to everyone? I wasn't the only Italian-descent kid in the class. But as my friends laughed I realized it wasn't the names. It was Grandma's stories I was retelling that made them all come alive.

Grandma's family, the D'Ippolitos, came from Palermo, Sicily and entered the United States at Ellis Island. Her father Giuseppe [Don Peppino] came over in 1902. He sent for his family to follow him

Opposite, above: Gertrude at her dining table. L-R: Gertrude, Margaret Periale D'Ippolito, Joseph Francis Periale, July 8, 1934. Below: Secundo "Parin" Cerchio and his family in 1910. [see page 128 for detailed caption].

[Parin]—shortening of the word for [Godfather] in Italian [Padrino], or Sicilian [Parrinu]. [Secundo]—Second, as in second son.

two years later. Gertrude's older siblings Francesco [19], Maria [16] and Filomena [15] came in February. Finally, in December of 1904 Gertrude arrived in America, age five, with her mother Giovannina and brothers Albert Settimo [8] and James Gabriel [9].

She always told the story that her name was entered on the rolls as Gertrude at Ellis Island by a clerk who couldn't spell Gaetana. Thanks to online genealogy I have discovered that might not be the whole story. She is recorded as Gaetana on the 1905 New York State Census [along with all of her family member's Italian names], but the census taker was an Italian. Another family story is that the nuns at school were the ones who changed her name.

Depolite Giuseppe	Head	m	30	44	Italy	3	?	Cook
Giovannina	Wife	w	7	43	Italy	1	al	Housework
Francisco	Son	m	m	19	Italy	2	al	Cook
Maria	Daughter	w	2	18	Italy	w	al	Garments
Filomena	Daughter	w	2	15	Italy	w	al	Garments
Giuseppino	Son	m	m	11	Italy	w	al	At School
Settimo	Son	m	m	8	Italy	w	al	At School
Gaetanina	Daughter	m	7	5	Italy	w	al	X

On the 1910 United States Census she is recorded as Gertrude, and her family's names have also all been Americanized: Joseph, Josephine, Frank, James, etc. The kids are all listed as being able to speak English, but the parents only Italian. Her family called her Tanina as a child, so Gertrude was able to keep a form of Gaetana as a nickname.

De Polito, Joseph	Head	M	W	49	M1	25			Italia	Italia	Italia	1901	Italia	owner	restaurant
Josephine	Wife	F	W	47	M1	25	6	6	Italia	Italia	Italia	1901	Italia	none	
Frank	Son	M	W	24	S				Italia	Italia	Italia	1901	English	cook	restaurant
James	Son	M	W	15	S				Italia	Italia	Italia	1904	English	none	
Filena	Daughter	F	W	13	S				Italia	Italia	Italia	1904	English	none	
Helen	Daughter	F	W	20	S				Italia	Italia	Italia	1904	English	none	
Gertrude	Daughter	F	W	11	S				Italia	Italia	Italia	1904	English	none	

I was horrified when I first heard the story of her losing her beautiful, musical name, but it was okay by Gertrude. She and her family wanted to be and sound American. After my father's death my brother and I discovered love letters in his belongings that were written by his parents to each other. Many from his father John Angelo Periale opened with "My beloved Gertie . . . " Seeing her adopted name in print, in his handwriting, helped.

D'Ippolitos

Giuseppe "Don Peppino" D'Ippolito
b: 1861 Palermo, Sicily
d: 1933 New York, NY

Giovannina Quartuccio
b: 1862 Piano dei Greci, Sicily
d: 1944 Belmar, NJ

Frank D'Ippolito
b: 1885 Sicily
d: c. 1974 Brooklyn, NY

Mary D'Ippolito
b: 1887 Marsala, Sicily
d: 1942 Glendora, NJ

Filomena "Fannie" D'Ippolito
b: 1889 Sicily
d: c. 1977 Bronx, NY

James Gabriel D'Ippolito
b: c. 1895 Sicily
d: c. 1916 New York, NY

Albert Settimo D'Ippolito
b: 1897 Marsala, Sicily
d: 1984 Jamaica, NY

Margaret Periale

Gaetana Marta "Gertrude" D'Ippolito
b: 1899 Marsala, Sicily
d: 1980 Belmar, NJ

John Angelo Periale

I grew up never knowing how to correctly pronounce my last name. The Americanized way to say Periale is [PAIR-ee-uhl]. Rhymes with burial—ugh. My brother likes to emphasize the last syllable [Pair—ee—ELL]. I asked Gertrude how Italians would pronounce it: [Payh—ree—AH—lay], and I pronounce it that way. I have since learned that in Piemontese, the dialect spoken in northern Italy where my grandfather's family was from, it would be pronounced [Pree—AHL]. What's in a name?

• •

The family always supported artistry. Gertrude's brother James Gabriel D'Ippolito was a painter who took classes at Cooper Union. I have a few of his surviving artistic efforts—two watercolors and a large pastel. He is listed as a tailor by occupation on the 1915 New York State Census. On the 1905 New York State Census older sisters Mary and Filomena [Fanny] were listed as workers in the garment district. Gertrude worked as a seamstress and later in life had her own bridal shop. I wonder if she learned to sew from her brother and her sisters, sewing being a skill most young women could use to earn a living. By Gertrude's account James was headstrong and temperamental and didn't take very good care of himself. He unfortunately died in 1916 at 21, of pneumonia. Family legend had him dying during the 1918 flu epidemic, but that didn't reach New York until September of that year.

James Gabriel and his brother Albert attended college at St. Joseph's School in Garden City. It was expensive for Don Peppino to send the two boys away to school on Long Island. The family decided that there wasn't enough money to also continue sending Gertrude to school at St. Patrick's downtown, just a few blocks away from Don Peppino's restaurant. So Gertrude never graduated high school. This new century yet old-world family still valued a boy's education over a girl's. With a chef for a father, James Gabriel and Albert received amazing boxes of food sent from home. Albert

Opposite: Watercolor by James Gabriel D'Ippolito, c. 1916 [signed J.J. D'Ippolito].

especially became quite a hit at college, his classmates eagerly anticipating mailings filled with such Sicilian delicacies as caponata, an eggplant relish.

don peppino's caponata

1 medium eggplant

1 cup black olives, 1 cup green olives

5 onions

1 pound of sliced tomatoes

2 tablespoons capers

3 stalks celery, diced

1/2 cup olive oil

1/3 cup vinegar

1 tablespoon sugar

Slice and dice eggplant in 1/2 inch squares. Slice and cube onions, sauté in 1/4 cup olive oil. When onions are golden, add tomatoes. Stir, then add rinsed capers, celery and pitted olives. Continue cooking until tomatoes are done. Remove pan from heat. Sauté eggplant in remaining 1/4 cup of oil, add to vegetables. Mix vinegar and sugar and pour over mixture. Toss. Serve hot or cold.

Opposite: Cabinet card of Gertrude's older sisters Mary D'Ippolito and Filomena "Fanny" D'Ippolito with their mother Giovannina Quartuccio D'Ippolito [seated], c. 1905.

Gertrude's version, which she called *caponatina,* had some slight variations from her father's recipe.

gertrude's caponatina

2 eggplants

2 cups chopped celery

1 jar of capers

2 jars [2lbs] Progresso Green Sicilian Olives [pit yourself]

2 cups of spaghetti sauce: 1 can paste plus 1 can peeled tomatoes, add 2-3 tablespoons wine vinegar, salt and pepper to taste

Peel eggplant. Slice into 1" thick cubes. Fry until soft, drain on brown paper. Chop celery, boil until slightly soft. Rinse capers to remove salt.

Combine all ingredients, mix in a glass or pottery bowl and refrigerate. Caponatina may be frozen! Serve as relish with pasta, especially lasgna or timbali, or with fish or meat.

Caponata, or *caponatina,* a family favorite, was frequently served at Gertrude's dinner table. It adds a nice addition to the main meal, as an appetizer or a side dish. It is *agrodolce* [sweet and sour], a feature of many Sicilian dishes. Caponata can be served as *primi piatti,* a first course, along with such dishes as olive *condite.* Our family usually served *caponata* at room temperature, as a relish.

I read that caponatina is the word for the dish when the vegetables are more finely chopped, but my uncle James Gabriel Periale told me that the dish is known as caponatina in Sicily and caponata in the rest of the world.

Opposite, above: Gertrude relaxes with the evening paper, 14th Street, New York, c. 1926. Below: Gertrude with lilacs in Manasquan, New Jersey, c. 1970.

cocktail hour

Pretzel rods, mixed nuts or little slices of cheddar cheese [no crackers] served with before-dinner cocktails—in my parents' case, usually a very dry Martini made with Gordon's gin, or a Manhattan.

One of the most delicious appetizers I have ever had, I had in Torino, when visiting some of my Italian relatives from the Periale side of my family—salvia fritta, fried sage leaves. The occasion where I first had them was a special one, in a very beautiful restaurant in Torino. The salvia fritta marked the beginning of a series of wonderful courses. I have always associated them with this sort of dining, which is far from my American grab-and-go eating experience. There is truly no reason not to make any meal special, so when I can fit them into the menu I do.

• •

salvia fritta

Wash several large sage leaves in cold water, drain and blot on paper towels. Beat one or two large eggs with a pinch of salt.

Mix dried bread crumbs in a large dish for the coating [some recipes use flour and water rather than eggs and bread crumbs, some no batter at all—give them all a try].

Heat some olive oil in a pan. Dip each leaf, first in the egg, then in the breadcrumbs, coating both sides. Place in hot oil and fry until golden brown. Drain on paper towel. Serve and enjoy.

Opposite: Wedding photo of Gertrude's sister Mary D'Ippolito and Joseph Battaglia, c. 1914.

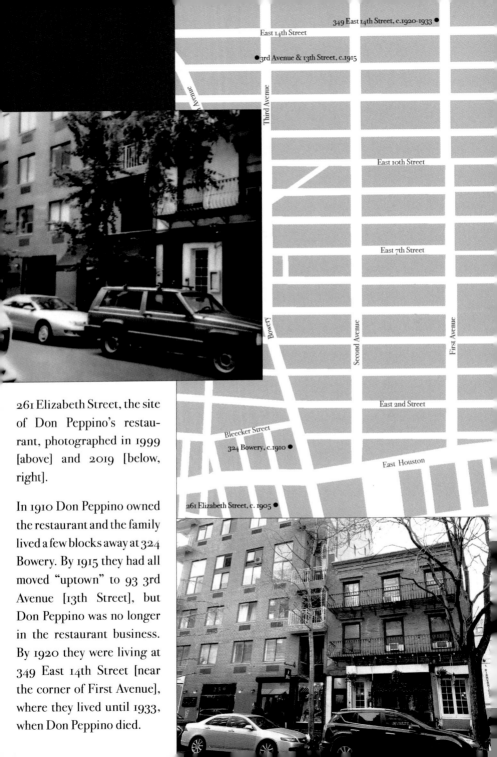

349 East 14th Street, c.1920-1933 ●

East 14th Street

● 3rd Avenue & 13th Street, c.1915

Third Avenue

East 10th Street

East 7th Street

Bowery

Second Avenue

First Avenue

East 2nd Street

Bleecker Street

324 Bowery, c.1910 ●

East Houston

261 Elizabeth Street, c. 1905 ●

261 Elizabeth Street, the site of Don Peppino's restaurant, photographed in 1999 [above] and 2019 [below, right].

In 1910 Don Peppino owned the restaurant and the family lived a few blocks away at 324 Bowery. By 1915 they had all moved "uptown" to 93 3rd Avenue [13th Street], but Don Peppino was no longer in the restaurant business. By 1920 they were living at 349 East 14th Street [near the corner of First Avenue], where they lived until 1933, when Don Peppino died.

Neither of Gertrude's parents, Giuseppe "Don Peppino" D'Ippolito nor his wife, Giovannina Quartuccio, spoke any English, only Sicilian. When Don Peppino came to America in 1902 he was listed on the ship's manifest as a cook. Family legend has him as a chef at the Ritz Carlton in New York before he sent for his family, who were still in Sicily, two years after his arrival in the United States. He may have worked there at some point in his restaurant career, but the famed hotel didn't open in Manhattan until 1911. Maybe his son Frank, also a chef, was the one who worked there.

Above: Wedding photo of Gertrude's sister Filomena "Fanny" D'Ippolito, who married Frank Battaglia in 1913.

Giovannina and three of their children [my grandmother the youngest, at five] arrived in America in 1904, a few months after Don Peppino became a naturalized citizen. They settled into their new life in Little Italy. In 1905 he was a cook at a restaurant on Elizabeth Street and the family lived in the same building. He was eventually able to buy the restaurant and operate it as his own.

After the First World War, Don Peppino decided to retire from the restaurant business and move uptown. His idea of uptown New York City was 14th Street.

Just because he retired, that didn't mean he stopped cooking. He continued to cook, but only on Sundays and holidays. Giovannina cooked the rest of the week. At home on a Sunday, Don Peppino would sit at the large round dinner table, holding court, while Giovannina brought dishes to him. He would sit for hours, preparing the food for the night's dinner.

Family memento: travel brochure for Taormina, Sicily.

When his prep work was done he would walk into the kitchen, to the big restaurant stove and work alone, a process taking several hours. When he finished he would untie his apron and return to the dinner table, resuming his previous position. Inside the kitchen there would be pots, pans and food everywhere. Giovannina would quietly clean up the mess. But what a feast he would prepare. Some of his specialties included *ricci di mare*, [pasta with sea urchins] and *babbaluci*, snails cooked in marinara sauce, both dishes from his native Sicily.

babbaluci

75 snails [in shell] in marinara sauce

2 28-ounce cans crushed tomatoes

2 tablespoons dried minced onion

6 garlic cloves, minced

1/4 cup chopped fresh parsley

1/2 cup carrot juice or 1/2 cup grated carrot

1 and 1/2 teaspoon dried basil

2 teaspoons oregano

2 teaspoons sugar

2 teaspoons salt, 1/4 teaspoon pepper

1 cup red wine

3 tablespoons olive oil

Combine all the ingredients and add snails, simmer for 1 and 1/2 hours to thicken sauce and flavor snails.

When Don Peppino retired he got "the calling." He became a healer. Many people would come to him for treatment—ranging from aches and pains to all manner of ailments. He would apply salves and the laying-on-of-hands to remove their ills. If anyone in their New York City Italian community felt out-of-sorts someone would say, "You must go and see Don Peppino, he will take care of you."

• •

Don Peppino's clients were predominantly Italians, traveling from all over the city and outskirts to his apartment on 14th Street to receive treatment. The family became used to frequent visitors coming to call and being ushered into Don Peppino's study. In the mid to late 1920s and early 1930s Italians living in the U.S. still spoke Italian primarily, not having much, if any, English. Gertrude liked to tell a story of how Don Peppino's treatments helped pave the way for her to meet her future husband, John Angelo Periale.

John Angelo lived in Paterson, in northern New Jersey, with his family. His mother, Paolina Cerchio Periale, had not been feeling well for some time and the Periales came to hear about Don Peppino. One day John Angelo brought his mother to the city for a consultation. Don Peppino spoke Sicilan and very little English, while Paolina spoke Piemontese. Don Peppino brought Gertrude into his study to help translate for him—Sicilian into English. Then John Angelo would translate English into Piemontese for his mother. Don Peppino initiated a series of treatments, which necessitated a series of visits to 14th Street. After his mother felt better, John Angelo kept coming by.

Opposite: On an outing, Paterson, New Jersey, c. 1920. Above: Albert D'Ippolito, Margaret Periale, Gertrude and John Angelo Periale. Below:, Gertrude and John Angelo Periale.

The always strict Don Peppino consented to him taking Gertrude out, with a condition: the two could go on double-dates with Gertrude's older brother Albert and John Angelo's younger sister Margaret as chaperones. Albert and Margaret weren't the best chaperones—they would frequently split off on their own, leaving John Angelo and Gertrude to get better acquainted. Not only did Gertrude and John Angelo fall in love and marry, in 1920, but Albert and Margaret ended up marrying also.

Don Peppino's most well-known treatment was the *Pumata*, the Green Salve. No one in the family is exactly sure of the recipe, but it is generally agreed that it contained quinine. It is believed that all the ingredients came from the local drugstore. Giovannina would boil and stir the mixture in a huge copper pot. They would make the *Pumata* in large quantities and then dispense it into old Noxzema jars, distributing it among the family and clientele as a cure-all. The combination of the salve and the healing application by Don Peppino made it a special treatment.

Above, left: Wedding photo of Margaret Periale and Albert D'Ippolito. Above, right: Gertrude and John Angelo Periale, c. 1920. Opposite: Don Peppino's parlor, 14th Street, New York, c. 1923. L-R: Unknown friend or relative, John Massimo Periale and Gertrude, reflected in mirror.

antipasti

An antipasto [literally, before the meal] is a slightly heavier dish than the aperitivo. It often consists of cured meats like salame, mortadella or prosciutto, served with cheeses and bread. A cold salmon dish or even bruschetta might be served.

After they were married, Gertrude and John Angelo and their four children—John Massimo, born in 1921, Joseph Francis [my father] born in 1925, Paula, born in 1927, and James Gabriel, born in 1932—lived with Don Peppino and Giovannina on 14th Street. The three boys were born in the apartment, with Paula born in Queens when the family lived there for a time.

• •

My uncle John Massimo adored his grandfather and told many stories about him and growing up on 14th Street. One of his favorites concerned a patient of Don Peppino's. Gertrude's brother Albert taught toddler John Massimo to stop crawling and stand up by playing a game: Albert would put a few pieces of candy in his coat pocket. Little John Massimo would pull himself up from the floor to reach into his uncle's coat pocket to get a treat . . . One hot summer day, a visitor arrived at the apartment. He left his coat in the hall and went into the nearby room where Don Peppino held his consultations. While Don Peppino was busy with his patient, John Massimo was crawling around the apartment. He made his way to the man's coat, which he had left draped over a chair outside Don Peppino's study. John Massimo pulled himself up and reached into the coat pocket and took out his prize—not candy this time, but a snub nosed .38 revolver.

He started to drag it down the hall, thumping it on the floor all the way. Gertrude's older sister Rose saw him and started screaming. The rest of the family ran out to see what had happened and quickly joined the uproar. Hearing all the commotion, Don Peppino came out of his study, the man right behind him and quickly sized up the situation. He turned to the man angrily and in Sicilian yelled at him, "What are you doing, bringing a "piece" into my home?" He told the man to leave and never come back again. The man was "one of the boys."

Opposite: Don Peppino's parlor, 14th Street, New York, New York, c. 1923.
Above: Gertrude with John Massimo Periale. Below: John Massimo Periale.

349 East 14th Street, photographed in the mid-1970s [above] and in 2019 [inset]. Don Peppino's office faced the street, with the family living in rooms towards the back of the building. The D'Ippolitos and Periales lived on two floors. The building originally had a stoop and the ground floor was a store that sold prosthetics and other medical supplies. Top photo: Mary Elizabeth Winship Periale and Elizabeth Anne Periale, standing in front of Allen's Bar.

While waiting for Don Peppino's Sunday feast there would always be something to nibble on. One of Don Peppino's favorite Sunday dinner appetizers to serve was poached salmon.

poached salmon

Serve this fish course right after the soup. Salmon would be a great choice.

Poach fish and make homemade mayonnaise.

Mix fish and mayonnaise and press into fish-shaped mold.

Use capers and thinly sliced carrots to represent fish scales.

Above: Double portrait of Gertrude, c. 1950.

olive condite

My family always had a jar of Progresso's Olive Condite on hand. It is sadly no more, but it could probably be replicated with the right ingredients: green olives, celery sliced thin, capers, thinly sliced red pepper, all marinated in olive oil, white wine vinegar and salt.

black olives

Gertrude's preferred were the canned jumbo black olives that have a meaty taste and work wonderfully on the tips of fingers for pointing and tossing across the table by my brother and me.

antipasto

So many things can be included. Red and green cherry papers, green and black olives. Rolled pieces of salami, mortadella, prosciutto, capicola. Marinated mushrooms, ceci and artichokes. Sliced provolone, mozzarella, chunks of parmesan and other cheeses. Grissini [bread sticks, with or without sesame seeds], sliced Italian bread. Hungry yet?

• •

Opposite, above: John Angelo Periale and Gertrude on Broadway, New York, c. 1930. Below: Joseph "Giuseppe" D'Ippolito, AKA Don Peppino, and his grandchildren, 14th Street, New York, c. 1930 [see page 135 for detailed caption].

[Ceci] - chickpeas. Gertrude loved to tell a story which has become Sicilian legend. During the War of the Vespers (1282) Sicilians expelled the Angevin French from their country. But how could one tell the difference between a Sicilian and a traitorous Frenchman? Hold up the humble chickpea and ask the person in question to name it. The French say the word with a soft consonant [seh-see] versus the Italian [cheh-chee]. The wrong pronunciation could prove fatal . . .

make sauce

Wed - make filling
provolone
muzzarella
salami   16 large muffins
prosciuto   12 small
meat Balls.   1 round large
milk & butter   1 small

Bring all ingredients
flour   sfinglcioni
olio-
butter   sfingscioni
meats   gèosi
yeast

                   Giogeor

My family spent many weekends at Gertrude's home throughout my childhood and there were numerous wonderful meals. But the best visits always seemed to be on holidays, when most of the rest of the family would come, and Gertrude would make our family's "specialty," sfincioni, and we'd all sit around the dinner table for hours and listen to stories and arguments and jokes.

In one of Gertrude's sfincioni shopping lists she plays with alternate spellings of the Sicilian Easter pie, which I've seen spelled sfingioni, sfinciuni. She always made a savory pie, with provolone, mozzarella, salami, prosciutto, meat balls, milk, butter, flour, yeast. From the list we can surmise that she was going to make her specialty at someone's house [I hope it was ours], as she was also bringing along 16 large muffin tins, 12 small, 1 large round and one small round cake pan—she must have been preparing a feast! I dimly recall a Christmas holiday when she had made little sfincioni muffins. They were delicious filled popovers.

When I was a child I thought sfincioni was a complete creation of Gertrude's. I have since learned that it is a variation on a popular Sicilian dish, pizza rustica, meaning country pizza. Pizza rustica is a filled pizza, or pie. Gertrude's version was a filled bread, a treat to be sliced and served warm, as an appetizer, while you were waiting for dinner.

sfincioni

Sfincioni is made with a brioche dough, with an egg wash on top. The two-crust dish is filled with provolone, mozzarella, salt and pepper in a béchamel sauce, mixed with finely chopped salami, prosciutto and sometimes tiny meatballs.

Opposite: Gertrude's sfincioni shopping list.

I have seen pizza rustica recipes with fillings that include sausage, pepperoni and ricotta., as wells as dessert pie recipes with raisins, cinnamon and walnuts in a sweet ricotta filling.

Everyone in our family makes a different version of sfincioni. John Massimo, Gertrude's oldest, probably came the closest to her perfection. His sister, my Aunt Paula, has made it with phyllo dough, like a savory turnover.

I have made pizza rustica with a braided top, much like a quiche, with a slightly sweeter dough than Gertrude's brioche.

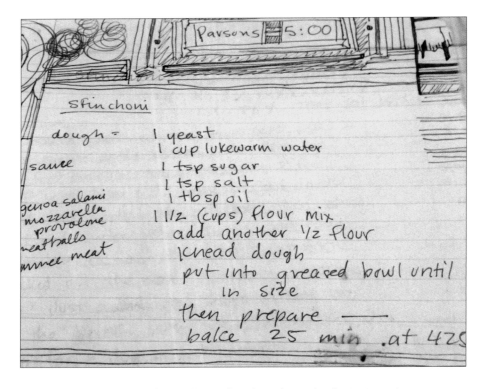

Above: I managed to get Gertrude to tell me how she made sfincioni one day, furiously scribbling down her ingredients and very minimal instructions. Opposite: Gertrude entered her Sicilian family delicacy in a Pillsbury baking contest, in 1962, but called it "Antipasto Tasty Loaf." I guess she thought that might be a less confusing name than Sfincioni. She didn't win, sadly. Philistines.

PILLSBURY'S $100,000 GRAND NATIONAL BAKE-OFF
OFFICIAL ENTRY BLANK. Contest closes June 30, 1962

Please Print: Mail to Pillsbury's Best Bake-Off, Box 673, Milwaukee 1, Wisc.

Name __Mrs. Gertrude M. Periale__

Address __302 Passaic Ave.__

City __Spring Lake__   Zone ____ State __New Jersey__

☐ JUNIOR (Any boy or girl 12 but not over 19 on March 1, 1962)
☐ SENIOR (anyone 19 or over on March 1, 1962)

CHECK TYPE OF RECIPE:

☐ Cakes   ☐ Cookies   ☒ Breads   ☐ Main Dishes   ☐ Pies   ☐ Desserts

BASIC RECIPE (dough, batter, or pastry):
If space is insufficient, use separate sheet and attach.

List below each ingredient and amount used in column indicated: FILLING, TOPPING, SAUCE, etc. (if necessary for serving):

AMOUNT	INGREDIENT	AMOUNT	INGREDIENT
	Dough		Filling
1/2 cup	milk scalded	1 cup	Salami
1/2 "	butter	1 "	Proscuitto
1 teaspoon	salt	1 "	Provoloni cheese
1 tablespoon	sugar	1 "	Mozzarella cheese
1 packet	active dry yeast		White Medium Sauce
1/4 cup	lukewarm water	2 tablespoons	"Pillsbury's Best All Purpose Flour"
1	egg	2 tablespoons	Butter
3	egg yolks well beaten	1 cup	milk
	save 1 tablespoon of yolks to brush dough		

Give Baking Temp. __425__ °F.   Baking Time __20 to 25 minutes__

NAME OF RECIPE __"Antipasto" Tasty Loaf__

I buy my flour from (list one store only) __The A & P market__

(1) Print your name and address. Give full directions on separate sheet and attach.
(2) Attach to this entry blank THE EXTRA-VALUE COUPON OR TRADE-MARK from any size package of Pillsbury's BEST Flour.

CONTEST CLOSES JUNE 30, 1962. ENTER NOW!

pizza rustica

dough:

2 and 1/2 cups all-purpose flour

1/2 cup granulated sugar

1/4 teasoon salt

1/2 teaspoon baking powder

10 tablespoons unsalted butter

1 egg

1/4 cup milk or water

Combine flour, sugar, salt and baking powder and add in butter. Beat egg with milk or water and stir into dry ingredients with a fork. Knead, shape, wrap in plastic and refrigerate until firm.

filling:

1/2 pound of mozzarella, thinly sliced or shredded

1/2 cup of grated romano and/or parmesan cheese

1/2 cup of shredded provolone cheese

3 eggs

1/4 teaspoon salt, 1/2 teaspoon freshly ground pepper

Whisk together cheeses, egg, salt and pepper.

Opposite: Above, Due fratelli–Unknown relatives from Palermo, Sicily [Don Peppino and his brother Andrea?]. Below, Don Peppino [?].

[Optional additions to the filling—tiny meatballs, salami, or cappicola ham, cut into little rectangles. Vegetarian options could include small sautéd mushrooms, onions, even spinach, although Gertrude never made it that way.]

Preheat oven to 350°. Butter a 9-inch round cake pan. Set aside a third of the dough. Roll out the remaining dough and line the pan, allowing dough to hang over the edge. Start spreading the filling in the pan. Add your meat or vegetable options and alternate layers with the filling. Roll out the remaining dough and cut into wide strips. Beat one more egg with a pinch of salt and paint the strips and the rim of the dough on the pan with the egg wash. Place the strips, criss-crossing over the pan. Press the strip edges into the dough on the side of the pan, trim excess dough, and press upward to create a rim. Bake for 45 minutes

It's very tasty, but as Gertrude would say, "Delicious, but not sfincioni!"

• •

After the sfincioni had been devoured and the dinner eaten and the coffee and the dessert served, everyone would remain seated at the dinner table. There would be an air of anticipation as we waited for the inevitable jokes and arguments, or, more politely put, "dynamic conversation." One person would start to tell a story while the coffee pot was being passed around the table after dinner. Everyone would react, editing and arguing, while wondering what would be served for dessert.

Opposite, above: Telling stories, Little Silver, New Jersey, July 25, 1979 [see detailed caption on page 135]. Below, Triumvirate: L-R: Albert D'Ippolito, Joseph Francis Periale and John Massimo Periale, at Gertrude's 80th birthday celebration, Little Silver, New Jersey, July 25, 1979.

As a child I got to see and learn a lot. About my family, about human behavior. And if I sat quietly enough, the grown-ups would forget I was sitting there and tell the juicier versions of their stories, while my brother John James and I tried to understand the punchlines of the racier jokes.

•　•

Gertude sometimes told stories about her parents. A favorite was a story from Don Peppino's childhood. When he was an altar boy in Palermo, Sicily, he and his friend Giovanni decided to have some fun. As churchgoers made their way outside after the service the two boys lingered and crept downstairs below the altar, to the catacombs beneath the church. They had a great time chasing each other through the tunnels, making echoes as they screamed at each other and the rats. Eventually they became bored and decided to head for home. They quickly realized that no matter where they walked, they never seemed to find the exit. Laughter soon changed to tears, as it seemed to get dimmer and darker around them. Above ground, chatting and socializing with their neighbors, their families finally noticed the little boys' absence and reentered the church to effect a rescue. They found the two little mischief-makers hugging each other, sobbing, in the center of the catacombs.

Opposite: Gertrude and family, c. 1937 [see page 135 for detailed caption].

Another favorite story—how her father became a chef. A teenage Don Peppino left home and worked as an apprentice galley boy in the maritime service. This was his first professional experience with cooking. As a young man, he worked throughout Italy in all manner of restaurants. He returned to Palermo to take a position as chef at the manor house of the local Duke. When the Duke and his family vacationed in England, they took Peppino with them. The ducal family wanted to keep him on in service, but Peppino, who was living in a very small room in the back of the servant's quarters, wanted a better life, so he started saving money to go to America.

• •

John Massimo adored his grandfather and would spend as much time with him as possible. Don Peppino liked to spend his evenings smoking cigars in his study. In the early evening he would rise from his chair, walk over to the window, throw it open and take a series of deep breaths. This was the only fresh air he got. He stored his cigar stubs in a box. When he collected enough stubs he would grind them and put them in his pipe—waste not, want not.

One cold February evening John Massimo was in the room with his grandfather when he rose to take his evening "airing." The window faced 14th Street and had a view of the front entrance of a speakeasy across the street. John Massimo joined his grandfather at the window. They watched a man come out of the speakeasy as a car pulled up, rapidly followed by three shotgun shots. Dazed, they stared as the man fell to the sidewalk and the front of the speakeasy was shot full of bullet holes. Don Peppino quickly pulled down the shade, pushed John Massimo down to the floor and turned off the lights. "You didn't see anything," he sternly told the boy. John Massimo checked the papers for weeks afterwards but there was never any mention of a murder . . .

• •

After he retired, Don Peppino would go to the meat-packing district, twice a year, on Easter and Christmas. John Massimo recalled his grandfather getting all dressed up in his best black suit, shoelace tie, Panama hat and cane. He would take little John Massimo along with him on the long walk across 14th Street, from the east side on First Avenue where they lived, to the west side of town, to the meat-packing district on 10th Avenue.

When Mr. Weinstein, Don Peppino's favorite butcher, saw him coming, he would rush out and welcome him. All the other butchers would run over and join them for a glass of wine that Mr. Weinstein had opened to honor his old friend. Don Peppino would order steaks and chops in large quantities, as if he still owned a restaurant. "Let me have 15 steaks, etc." When John Massimo and his grandfather returned home and the meat was delivered, Giovanna would shake her head and they would have to give a lot of the food away to friends and neighboring family.

Opposite: John Massimo Periale, c. 1931.

primi

Primi is the first course. Risotto, gnocchi, soup, lasagne, pasta or broth are all common dishes.

Don Peppino died at the onset of the Depression, in 1933, and the family fortunes went downhill after his death. The family had to leave 14th Street. They moved to the Bronx, living in very close quarters and reduced financial circumstances. John Angelo answered an ad in the paper, soon after Pearl Harbor, for a job developing radar. He commuted from the Bronx to Belmar, New Jersey, to Camp Evans, where the job was based. By February 1942, he moved the family permanently to the Jersey Shore.

• •

Don Peppino wasn't the only person featured in family stories. Gertrude's mother Giovannina Quartuccio had been married before. Her husband, a stone mason surnamed Cosentino, was mistreating her. A man from the town where Giovannina was living came to their town in Sicily, not far from Palermo, and and told them that they better come and look at their daughter. Her mother Filomena Maisano and her father Giacomo Quartuccio, also a mason [and a card player and gambler] rushed to rescue her when they heard of her plight. She was six months pregnant and, luckily for him, her husband was away when they arrived. Filomena and Giacomo told all of the neighbors that they were taking their daughter home and they better never lay eyes on the husband again. She must have been divorced or the marriage annulled. A few years later Giovannina met Giuseppe D'Ippolito [Don Peppino] and they were married and raised her son Frank Cosentino as their own. They went on to have six children together: [another] Frank, Mary, Filomena [Fanny], James Gabriel, Albert Settimo and Gaetana Marta [Gertrude]. When the D'Ippolitos emigrated to America, Frank Cosentino stayed in Italy, but he did come to visit the family in New York.

Opposite: L-R, Rose Anzalone Periale, Gertrude, James Gabriel Periale, Joseph Francis Periale and Giovannina Quartuccio D'Ippolito [the only photo I have of her], Belmar, N.J., c. 1942.

Gertrude loved to tell a story about her mother Giovannina's grandfather, Francesco. When Giovannina's paternal grandfather Giacomo Quartuccio's mother [Giovanna Norcia] died, his father, Francesco married again—a widow with five or six children. Francesco died soon after, leaving the widow with everything—his money, his possessions. His family was outraged. They believed that according to Italian law, the land and the house should have gone to Giacomo, the first-born son.

According to family legend the widow stole everything while they were all attending Francesco's funeral—hiding all of Francesco's hard-earned money under her mattress. The family tried to reclaim this land, but were never successful. Giacomo's wife Filomena exacted revenge in her own manner. She would wait until harvest time and then go and take her pick of the harvest off of her deceased father-in-law's land. If this story is accurate, the family held this grudge against the "evil widow" a long time—long enough for Giacomo, who was ten years old when his father died, to grow up and marry Filomena. Gertrude had another strange variation on this legend: the "evil widow" died in a fire and they found all the money under the bed burnt with her.

• •

At my Uncle John Massimo's house the food was served to us practically before we walked in the door. We would be hustled to the kitchen table and immediately offered a seat, where we would listen to and trade stories and reminiscences, killing time until the table in the dining room was set for dinner. If we were there for a weekend visit, we knew to leave room for multiple courses and adjust our belts, as the food was guaranteed not to stop coming until we left [with leftovers packed up to go].

Opposite: Dinner at Gertrude's, Spring Lake, New Jersey, c. 1979 [see page 136 for detailed caption].

When I was in college at Parsons School of Desgn in New York, far away from my family in South Jersey, I really got to know my Aunt Rose, John Massimo's wife, who insisted that I come visit any weekend that I didn't have something else to do or was going home to Jersey. And I did. Uncle John would pick me up at the L.I.R.R. station, and as soon as I crossed the threshold of their home a plate of food would come my way and the stories would start. She and I would sit at that table for hours shooting the breeze until Uncle John would get restive and come in and take over. Aunt Rose was a great cook, but while I visited John Massimo was in charge of the kitchen and would cook the evening's main course, usually a roast of beef or turkey. Aunt Rose would whip up a quick snack to tide us over until dinner. "You look so thin! Want a tomato sandwich? What? Your mother never made you a tomato sandwich?!" One of her favorite go-tos was the Italian-American lunch classic.

• •

tomato sandwiches

As delicious as they are simple, the perfect summer [or anytime] sandwich.

2 slices of your favorite bread.

1 medium Jersey beefsteak tomato, perfectly ripe, cut in horizontal slices.

Lots of mayonnaise.

Salt and coarsely ground black pepper.

You can toast the bread or add a slice of cheese if you like, but a pure tomato sandwich is the best.

Opposite: John Massimo Periale and Rose Anzalone Periale c. 1942.

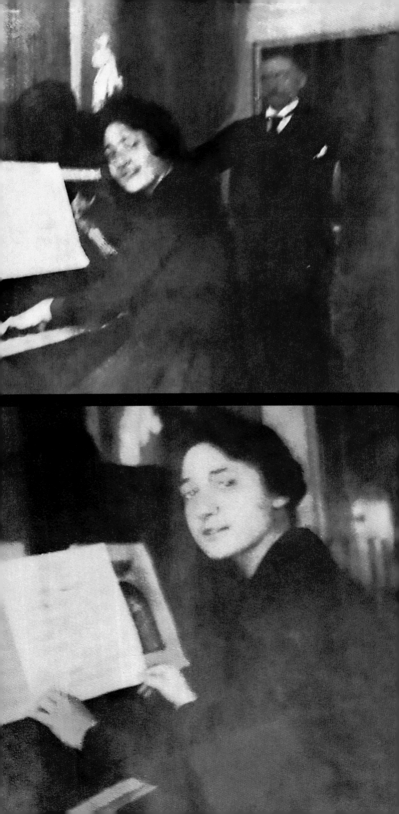

Gertrude learned a lot of her recipes from her father, but her mother Giovannina was quite a cook in her own right. Opinions differ on where they heard she was from: Albania [Cousin Judith], Malta [Aunt Paula], Grecia Romana [Uncle Jim], or Magna Grecia [my mom]. I have discovered that Giovannina Quartuccio was from Piana dei Greci, where all of the Quartuccios hailed from. Piana dei Greci [now called Piana dei Albanesi] is about 24 km south of Palermo, in Sicily. It was originally settled in the late 15th and early 16th century by Albanians and Greeks. So everyone was a little bit right about her origins. Giovannina like to attend service at the Greek Orthodox church when she lived in New York and her cooking had a decidedly Greek influence. She was apt to include lemons in many of her dishes. One of her favorite recipes was a fish soup.

• •

giovannina's fish soup

Whitefish, whole, put in large soup pot. A whole head of garlic, big handful of fresh parsley, sautéed whole onion, lots of pepper. Remove fish from pot after cooking for an hour, debone, put meat back into pot. Right before serving, squeeze the juice of a whole lemon into the pot. Variations: crush and drop angel hair pasta into soup. Add one whole egg, stirring quickly. Sometimes Giovannina would marinate the fish flesh and they would make a salad with it.

Opposite: Gertrude at the piano, with Joseph "Giuseppe" D'Ippolito, AKA Don Peppino, looking on, New York, New York, c. 1919.

Giovannina didn't want to leave the city after Don Peppino's death, so she stayed in the Bronx with some cousins. She got a bad case of flu and was admitted to Bellevue Hospital. A close family friend, Pete DiPeri [the husband of Gertrude's greatest friend, May Mahler], contacted Gertrude and told her he would bring her home from the hospital to live with them in New Jersey. When Pete, who ran a funeral parlor in New York, picked her up he and his assistant were sitting up front in his company vehicle—a hearse. Would she mind riding in the back? Giovannina, definitely a good sport, agreed. She was grateful to be getting home to her family. She laughed all the way down to Belmar, as the two men regaled her with jokes and stories. Gertrude's next door neighbor almost had an apoplexy watching them *unload* a hearse.

• •

Gertrude got her love of opera from her mother. Giovannina was musical and played the piano. She also liked to play operas on the Victrola and sing along to them. Was it true that Gertrude wanted to be an opera singer but her father Don Peppino, wouldn't let her? Yes. He was an old-world gentleman. He didn't think such a career was dignified or proper for a young girl. At least that is how I first heard the story, from Gertrude herself, but there is another version: Gertrude gave up singing lessons because of her fresh piano teacher. According to my aunt Paula, Gertrude's daughter: Gertrude took singing lessons. She was apparently so good and had such a range that at one of these lessons, after hitting all the high notes, her teacher was overcome by her talent and grabbed her and kissed her on both cheeks and embraced her. She was horribly embarrassed and when she told her parents Don Peppino informed her that was her last lesson.

Family stories tell moments in the lives of people you love from a time when you didn't know them. These tales are told slightly differently each time. Or differently by different people.

Opposite: Gertrude's opera libretto of "Lakme," by Léo Delibes.

METROPOLITAN OPERA HOUSE

GRAND OPERA

GIULIO GATTI-CASAZZA
GENERAL MANAGER.

LIBRETTO

THE ORIGINAL ITALIAN,
FRENCH OR GERMAN
LIBRETTO WITH A
CORRECT ENGLISH
TRANSLATION.

LAKME

FRED. RULLMAN, Inc.

17 EAST 42nd STREET, NEW YORK CITY
THE ONLY CORRECT AND AUTHORIZED EDITION
KNABE PIANO USED EXCLUSIVELY

PRINTED IN U.S.A.

Maybe Gertrude lost her opportunity to pursue a career in opera, but she always loved music. I can remember hearing her sing along to the Metropolitan Opera on the radio on Sundays. Especially Puccini. She loved the most dramatic stories, like *La Forza del Destino* and *Tosca*.

Above: Elizabeth Anne Periale with Gertrude, Sea Girt, New Jersey, c. 1968.

When Gertrude would make us lunch it would usually include a tasty soup.

lentil soup

1 cup dried lentils, rinsed thoroughly

6 cups chicken or vegetable stock

1 cup crushed canned tomatoes [tomato sauce or paste also works—use whatever is in your pantry]

4 tablespoons extra virgin olive oil

1 large yellow onion, 3 large stalks celery, 2 large carrots, diced

2-3 cloves finely minced garlic

1 tablespoon dried basil, 1 teaspoon dried oregano

1/2 teaspoon freshly ground black pepper, sea salt to taste

Optional: add 1/2 cup white wine or sherry to the broth. Heat oil in a large pot. Add the diced onions, celery and carrots and sauté until tender and the onions are golden in color. Add the garlic and wine and let simmer for a minute. Add the stock, tomatoes and lentils. Cover and simmer for approximately 45 minutes or until the lentils are tender. Add the parsley, basil, oregano, dill, freshly ground black pepper and salt to taste. Garnish with grated Parmesan, if desired.

Other soups Gertrude liked: She made her own version of Italian Wedding/Chickarina soup, a chicken broth with vegtables like carrots and escarole, tiny meatballs and acini di pepe [pasta pearls, literally "peppercorns"]. "A nice consommé" was always a great choice for a light lunch.

le paste

Gertrude's favorite pasta was cavatelli, a pasta popular in Sicily. She called them little boats, although the name in Italian literally means "little hollows."

She mostly cooked spaghetti [little strings], a popular pasta from Sicily, probably the most popular when I was a kid in the '70s.

I don't remember her ever cooking angel hair or linguini or any other long pasta apart from long fusilli, my father's favorite, which she made for him often when we were at her house for Sunday dinner.

My favorite pasta shapes are conchiglie [shells] and mostaccioli [little mustaches] rigati—little tubes cut at an angle with rigati [lines or ridges].

Gertrude always served pasta with marinara sauce. She never made white sauce or pesto or bolognese. Or put things like mushrooms or spinach in her sauce. Vegetables were served on the side. But she did make meatballs.

• •

One Thanksgiving Gertrude and my mom planned to serve a turkey. The dinner was being cooked at our house, and Gertrude would stay the weekend. Somehow they forgot to either defrost the bird or turn on the oven, so we ended up having spaghetti. Spaghetti on Thanksgiving became a tradition for me as an adult.

spaghetti and meatballs

1 pound spaghetti

1 pound ground beef

1/3 cup bread crumbs

1/4 cup finely chopped parsley

1/4 cup freshly grated Parmesan + more for serving

1 egg

2 garlic cloves, minced

2 tablespoons extra-virgin olive oil

1/2 cup onion, finely chopped

1 28-ounce can crushed tomatoes

1 bay leaf

Salt and freshly ground black pepper

In a large pot of boiling salted water, cook spaghetti according to package instructions. Drain. In a large bowl, combine beef with bread crumbs, parsley, Parmesan, egg, garlic, salt [optional: a pinch of red pepper flakes]. Form into 16 balls. In a large pot over medium heat, heat oil. Add meatballs and cook, turning occasionally, until browned on all sides, about 10 minutes. Transfer meatballs to a plate. Add onion to pot and cook until soft, 5 minutes. Add crushed tomatoes and bay leaf. Season with salt and pepper and bring to a simmer.

Variations to spaghetti sauce: sometimes Gertrude would throw in a sliced carrot, which would dissolve as the sauce cooked and sweeten it slightly. Variations to meatballs: "Meatball Surprise"—sometimes she would insert a little piece of mozzarella inside the meatball.

Above: Periale ladies at the beach, c. 1921. L-R: Della Periale Himadi, Paola Cerchio Periale, Margaret Periale D'Ippolito and Ernie Periale Gillia.

My uncle James Gabriel Periale makes a baked pasta, based on one of his mother Gertrude's recipes:

pasta al forno/timballo

2 boxes of mostaccioli pasta

2-3 medium size eggplants

Parmesan and Pecorino Romano cheese

1 and 1/2 pounds mozzarella

Tomato Sauce

1 package of mushrooms

1 and 1/2-2 pounds ground beef [optional]

1 package frozen peas

3-4 tablespooons pine nuts

Olive oil

Butter

Bread crumbs

Handful of parsley

Brown the ground meat and sliced mushrooms separately and set aside. Peel and slice eggplant, lengthwise, in 1/2" thick slices. Fry in shallow pan until uniformly brown, drain and stack on brown paper and set aside.

Opposite: James Gabriel Periale, Bronx, New York, c. 1938.

[Pasta al forno] - pasta cooked in the oven

[Timballo] - kettledrum

Cook pasta, rinse in cold water and set aside while you prepare the assembly of the timballo.

Grease an aluminum or enamel roasting pan with butter and then coat the pan evenly with breadcrumbs. Layer the ingredients in the pan as follows: pasta, grated cheese, a thin coating of sauce, mushrooms, meat and peas, pine nuts, eggplant [3-4 slices to cover].

Repeat the layering 2-3 times, until ingredients are 3/4" below top edge of pan. Finish layering with pasta, sauce, and a

topping of bread crumbs. Cover and refrigerate while preheating the oven to 350°F. Bake, covered, for an hour. Uncover and bake an additional 15 minutes. Turn off oven but let timballo continue to bake 15 more minutes. Remove from oven and let cool for 10 minutes. Using a knife, release the edge of the pasta from the edge of the pan. Place a serving dish over the pan, holding firmly and invert. Remove pan and garnish with breadcrumbs and parsley. Serve and enjoy.

Above: John Angelo Periale, c. 1916. Opposite: John Angelo Periale and Gertrude c. 1943.

Cooking helped my grandparents keep their family traditions alive. John Angelo's family spoke Piemontese and Gertrude's Sicilian, so they spoke English to each other. They were a truly American couple.

When John Angelo and Gertrude moved their family to New Jersey they were also moving closer to John Angelo's family, which meant that their family was also introduced to a whole new style of food—northern Italian cuisine. John Angelo occasionally persuaded Gertrude to make a few Piemontese dishes, but for the most part she stayed with what she knew and what she learned from her parents. John Angelo would cook northern Italian family dishes, like risotto with chicken livers and Gertrude would make eggplant parmigiana and other southern delicacies. Every once in a while John Angelo would insist on having one of his favorite childhood dishes, especially polenta.

Polenta, cornmeal mush, is a northern Italian pasta substitute. The best time for John Angelo to make polenta would be after Gertrude had cooked a roast. He would chop what meat was left over from the roast into small 1/4 inch cubes, trimming off all the fat, and make gravy. Then he would make the polenta.

Above: Periales and Cerchios in Lodi, New Jersey, c. 1925 [see page 136 for detailed caption].

Periales

Massimo Periale
b: 1858 Torino, Italy
d: 1939 Paterson, NJ

Paola Cerchio
b: 1863 Torino, Italy
d: 1924 Lodi, NJ

Carolina "Lena" Periale
b: 1884 Torino, Italy
d: 1948 New Hyde Park, NY

Rose Periale
b: 1886 Torino, Italy
d: 1972 Vallejo, CA

Ernesta "Ernie" Periale
b: 1887 Torino, Italy
d: 1972 NY

Adelaide "Della" Periale
b: 1890 Torino, Italy
d: 1973 Boca Raton, FL

Frank Joseph Periale
b: 1891 New York, NY
d: 1918 Bergen, NJ

John Angelo Periale
b: 1896 Paterson, NJ
d: 1951 Belmar, NJ

Gaetana Marta "Gertrude"
D'Ippolito

Margaret Periale
b: 1898 NJ
d: 1983 Jamaica, NY

Albert Settimo
D'Ippolito

polenta

In a medium-size pot mix 2 cups cornmeal with 3 cups cold water. Add this mixture to 3 cups boiling water. Stir with a cucciata [wooden spoon]. Spread polenta out on a big platter or, more traditionally, a large wooden board. The polenta can be left to set and then cut into squares.

• •

The way John Angelo liked to serve polenta was to pour the gravy over the whole platter. He would then encourage everyone to reach into the center of the table and spoon a great big serving onto their plates. They only made his favorite dish once this way because Gertrude did not like serving it in the "peasant" manner. John Angelo thought of it all as fun. It was communal and reminded him of his childhood. He was a playful person and offset Gertrude's more serious, sometimes rigid side. When Gertrude made polenta for John Angelo she would place a spoonful of the cornmeal neatly into bowls and ladle a dollop of gravy on top, serving it with a vegetable on the side. Another aspect of the polenta-making process that didn't thrill Gertrude was the mess it made out of her pots, as it adhered to whatever pot or pan she was using like glue.

I have made polenta with sausage: sauté onions, garlic, mushrooms, green peppers in a pan with olive oil. Add some sweet Italian sausage, cook together until sausage is done. Pour over polenta. Frankly, I'm with Gertrude on this one. It takes forever to scrape the remnants of the mush out of the pots. I prefer the above mixture ladled over pasta.

Opposite: Gertrude's cookbook, held together by ribbon, contained a few sheets with dashed off ingredients that we can piece together like archaeology to recreate her recipes. [The Century Cook Book, by Mary Ronald, 1901].

[Cucchiaio]—spoon in Italian. My family is likely using a dialect version for [cucciata], which literally means [kennel] in Italian.

MARY RONALD'S
CENTURY
COOK
BOOK

As she got older Gertrude would take the the usual cooking short-cuts, including store-bought tomato sauce. But she taught me a trick to make my pasta sauce special, no matter whether I was making it from scratch or pressd for time and using a jar from the store— add the oregano at the end of the process and crush the leaves as you sprinkle them into the sauce to bring out the herb's flavor—rubbing flakes between one's palms works well.

When she still lived on 14th Street Gertrude would watch her father Don Peppino make a delicious sun-dried tomato sauce. In the summertime he would go up to the roof of their apartment building and stretch a fine mesh screen over the top of a barrel. He would set ripe tomatoes on the screen to dry for hours in the sun. When the tomatoes were ready, he would mash the tomatoes, pressing them through the mesh of the screen. The sauce would drip into the large pot he had set inside the barrel below his homemade sieve/drying rack.

don peppino's tomato sauce

After making a beef roast on Sunday he would save the gravy and drippings to make a wonderful tomato sauce,

Deglaze the pan with olive oil and chop some bacon and on-ions—about the size of a horse's teeth [!] Brown the onions, bacon and garlic. Add peeled tomatoes, a little bit of sugar, salt, pepper, basil, oregano, 1/2 can of tomato paste, 1 can of water, Simmer one hour.

John Angelo's father Massimo was a baker and, more importantly, a family legend. At the age of eleven his family in northern Italy [Piedmont, Torino], wanted him to become a priest. His father was a school teacher who played the organ at the local church and was known as The Professor. But Massimo did not want to be a priest. He ran off and crossed the Italian border into Switzerland. He soon became hungry, and catching the delicious smell of baking bread, walked into a bakery. The couple who owned it were childless and took him in and trained him as a baker. He eventually returned to Torino, opened his own bakery, and met and married Paolina Cerchio.

Above: Paolina Cerchio Periale visits her brother Nicola Cerchio's family in Wilmington, Delaware, 1915 [see page 138 for detailed caption].

Paolina was also from Torino. She told Gertrude many stories about her father Parin's brother, "Daddy's Mother's Uncle," called Barbarossa. Barbarossa not only had an impressive name, but also an imposing frame—he was such a large man that he would fill the doorway as he entered any room.

In Torino, which was located in the province of Savoy, Barbarossa had an altercation with another military officer who was taunting him. Barbarossa almost killed the man—he threw him down a ladder which led up to one of the parapets of the fort where they were stationed. He was sentenced to 50 lashes, which was equivalent to a death sentence. His family had some influence and was able to get him off with only 10 lashes. Barbarossa was brought back to his cell, where he wrote an eloquent letter to La Duchessa Adelaide of the region of Savoy. La Duchessa was so touched by Barbarossa's eloquent and poetic letter she granted his release. He later fought for England in the Crimean War [probably c. 1855 when Piedmont entered the war]. Years later he met and married a woman named Margaret. John Angelo's younger sister Margaret was named after her and his older sister Della was named after Duchessa Adelaide.

Another Periale family story featured Barba Filip [short for Filippo], who was said to have been Massimo's brother and may have paved the way for the Periale family to come to America.

Opposite: Paolina Cerchio Periale, 1910.

[Barbarossa]—literally [barba rossa, red beard] in Italian. [Barba] is also Piemontese for [uncle] so his nickname was a play-on-words.

Crimean War—1853-1856.

Duchy of Savoy—[1416–1860] included parts of France, western Italy and southwestern Switzerland. The House of Savoy led the unification of Italy in 1861 and ruled the Kingdom of Italy from 1861 until 1946.

The Duchessa of Savoia in 1855 was Adelaide of Austria, wife of Vittorio Emanuele Maria Alberto Eugenio Ferdinando Tommaso di Savoia, who was Duke of Savoy from 1849-1861 and then King of Italy from 1861-1878.

[Barba Filip]—Piemontese for [Uncle Phil].

Filippo fell in love with a local rich girl. The two young lovers planned to elope, but her brothers came after them to prevent the marriage. There was a fight and Filippo killed one of the girl's brothers. Massimo may have been a Mercutio in this Romeo and Juliet scenario. There is a version of the story where both he and his brother had to flee Italy, leaving Europe through The Netherlands on two different ships—Massimo to the United States and Filippo to South America. The family never heard from Filippo again, but recently through social media I have been in contact with some Periales in Chile and Argentina. The description of Filippo closely resembles Barbarossa—he was also a very large man with red hair.

Massimo married Paolina around 1884. They had four daughters by 1890: Lena, Rose, Ernie and Della. Massimo may have left on a boat for America from Rotterdam before sending for his family, but I have been unable to find a record of this trip or Filippo's. *La Bretagne* is the ship Massimo and his family sailed on in March of 1891. The ship's manifest lists Massimo, Paola, and daughters Lena, Rose, and Ernie all bound for America together. Family legend says Massimo went to America and was living with a Dutch girl and her family that he had met on the boat. Time passed with no word from Massimo, so Paola's father Parin set off for America to find and bring back his wayward son-in-law. But I could only find Parin on a ship's manifest from 1893, his occupation listed as shoemaker, emigrating at age 59 to Paterson, New Jersey, two years after Massimo and Paolina and family arrived.

• •

Another family legend: Massimo and Paolina's daughter Della, still a baby, was left behind with a wet-nurse in Italy. There are varying stories as to why she might not have joined them when they emigrated to the United States. One reason given was that with the family running a business [the Periale Bakery] Paolina wouldn't be able to nurse her baby, so they gave the infant to another family to raise

Opposite: 1922 Calendar from Periale & Sons French Bakers, 27 East Place, Lodi, New Jersey.

FERRIS & SONS

FRENCH BAKERS

27 East Place   Lot. N 7

1922	MAY				1922
SUN	MON	TUE	WED	THU	FRI	SAT
	1	2	3	4	5	6
7	8	9	10	11	12	13
14	15	16	17	18	19	20
21	22	23	24	25	26	27
28	29	30	31			

and paid for her keep. Another story had her staying in Italy and living with a family as a domestic—but she would have had to have been much older, at least a teenager. On the 1900 U.S. Census Della is recorded as living with her family in New Jersey, age 10. That document also states she had been in the U.S. for ten years . . . The *La Bretagne* manifest also lists a baby named Adele in steerage, but with a different family. Maybe wet nurse and baby Della were listed in a different section of steerage from her family and older siblings . . . Massimo and Paola had three more children, all born in the United States: Frank, Margaret and John Angelo, my grandfather.

• •

John Angelo's sister Della was a true American success story. She became an entrepreneur in the pharmaceutical industry with her husband, Dr. Daoud "David" Himadi. A favorite family story centered around Della and her brand new car—a Cadillac. One day Della and her husband came to visit her father Massimo and family in Lodi, N.J. After everyone dutifully admired their gorgeous vehicle Himadi put the car in the barn, so it wouldn't get dusty or dirty. They all moved inside to visit and soon sat down to eat. John Angelo fidgeted restlessly at the dinner table. He could think of nothing but that brand new Cadillac and how it was sitting, unattended, in the barn. He was finally allowed to excuse himself from the table. He headed quietly and swiftly out to the barn.

After dessert Della and her husband said their goodbyes and went to retrieve their car. Himadi opened the door to discover the Cadillac—in pieces—spread all over the barn floor. John Angelo, always fascinated to see how things worked, had taken it apart. Himadi saw red. Massimo stepped between them, "Now wait a minute." He turned to John Angelo, "Take those shafts down off the wall, put the wheels back onto the Cadillac and put a horse in front of it and. ride it down to the blacksmith's and watch him put it back together. You'll know what to do next time!"

Opposite: Paolina Cerchio Periale and her daughters, c. 1910 [see page 138 for detailed caption].

• •

The family mostly ate Gertrude's pasta, but when visiting Della, everyone would make gnocchi together.

gnocchi with cheese

3 large potatoes

1 egg

Salt and freshly ground black pepper

1 cup all-purpose flour + more for dusting

2 tablespoons butter

Freshly grated Parmigiano-Reggiano cheese

Ground nutmeg

Preheat oven to 350°F. Place potatoes, sliced down the center, on a baking sheet. Bake until very tender, 1 hour–1 hour and 30 minutes. As soon as they are cool enough to handle, peel and discard skins. Use a potato ricer or mash into a bowl. Mix in egg, salt and flour–enough to make the dough workable but not too sticky. On a floured surface divide dough evenly into four sections. Roll each section into a 3/4-inch-thick rope and cut into 3/4-inch-long pieces. Roll each piece into a ball, then flatten into a circle.

Bring a large pot of salted water to a boil. Add gnocchi. Stir gently until gnocchi rise to surface–about 4-5 minutes.

Opposite: Della Periale Himadi, age 28, with son David Himadi in 1918 [see page 140 for detailed caption].

81

PUSHED A BALKY HORSE

A Colonel, a Doctor and a Gang of Street Arabs Pushed the Nag for Blocks.

Considerable amusement was occasioned at the corner of Main street and Hamilton avenue yesterday morning, when a horse, attached to a baker's wagon and driven to a standstill by a boy driver, refused absolutely to move a step further.

All sorts of schemes and devices were used to start the animal, but without success. An abundance of gratuitous advice was handed out from the crowd of onlookers.

Colonel Shelby, of the animal society, was early on the job, as were Dr. W. J. Reagan and Oscar Korten, also officers of the society.

The doctor said it was the "dumb staggers." Dumb it certainly was, but "staggers," not much. A locomotive could have hardly caused it to stagger; and for downright stubbornness the animal had the army mule relegated back to the lemon class.

"Tickle 'im with a baseball bat," volunteered one urchin. The colonel, by this time, no doubt would have liked to, but wasn't he an officer of the S. P. C. A? And, besides, a short while before he had stopped the driver from using his whip on the animal, so he contented himself with giving the lad a look that caused him to fear for his safety, and he slowly evaporated.

Coaxing, petting, tempting with sweets, threats and other methods were without avail. "Build a fire under him," suggested a citizen, rather facetiously.

Finally a bright idea hit the resourceful colonel. "We'll push 'in along," says Shelby, and the crowd, ready for more fun, concluded it was a good thing and needed helping along.

The animal was unhitched and Mr. Shelby and Dr. Reagan began the pushing process. About forty urchins gathered behind in a long line, two by two, hands on each others backs and shoulders, and with Messrs. Shelby and Reagan leading and backed by the united strength of the forty odd urchins, pushing the flanks of the animal, progress was made slowly but surely.

After about fifteen minutes of this work, the animal was pushed as far as Washington street and Hamilton avenue, but the crowd had tired of the pushing game and a new method must be sought.

From a nearby stable a rope was secured, and this was used as a tackle and placed about the body of the refractory animal. A team of horses was then secured and a hauling process was begun. This was more effective and the animal was soon hauled into Secor's stable, where it remains at present, in the care of a veterinary surgeon.

It was learned that the horse was the property of M. Periale, a baker, of Slater and Pine streets. The horse had been driven since 3 a. m. and was afflicted with the "dumb staggers." It will be bled this morning, and the surgeons say this will cure it.

Another horse fell yesterday in front of the police station and cut its mouth. Colonel Shelby objected to the driver's treatment of the fallen animal and several citizens "butted in" and interfered with the officer's performance of his duty.

OPPOSITION TO

Transfer to a casserole dish with a slotted spoon, draining off any excess water. In a skillet over medium-high heat, melt butter. Carefully transfer cooked gnocchi to skillet, adding 3 tablespoons of the cooking liquid. Stirring constantly, cook until a creamy and loose butter sauce forms and coats gnocchi—about one minute. Remove from heat, and season with cheese, salt and pepper to taste. Sprinkle each serving with grated cheese and nutmeg. Serve immediately.

• • • • • • • • • • • • • • •

The family moved to Lodi, New Jersey and Massimo opened a bakery. The Periale Bakery was not a storefront. It was a bread delivery service. Massimo would go out with the horse and wagon on Saturday morning to deliver bread and to collect accounts from the stores and homes that were his clients. Quite often by 6 pm he hadn't returned home. Paolina would become worried and ask John Angelo to go out and see if he could find his father. Ten minutes after he left the house John Angelo would see the horse coming up the road, leading a seemingly empty wagon. Massimo would be laid out in the back, drunk. John Angelo would bring the horse and cart into the barn. Sometimes Massimo would get up and come into the house.

82

Sometimes John Angelo would leave him there and he would sleep it off. No matter how often this happened Paolina would always get worried and ask John Angelo to go out and look for his father.

• •

One wintry February Massimo was laid up with a cold, so Paolina had to take care of any customers who might call. One day a Mrs. Martini came by to pay her bill. Paolina knew that Massimo kept an account book with all the customer's names in it. She found a black bound book behind the counter and opened it to look up her account. She flipped hrough it, turning redder and redder with each page's turning. She finally closed the book and told Signora Martini that she'd better come back another time when her husband was feeling better.

She went upstairs, the book tucked under her arm, and marched into their bedroom where Massimo lay fast asleep and hit him hard over the head with it. He woke up, shouting, "What's the matter with you?"

She answered, "What's this?" and tossed the book at his head. He ducked, laughing. The book had fallen open to "Signora Martini, *la putana con la culla grande.*" Massimo's method of keeping accounts was to use very descriptive phrases for his more difficult customers, such as "ugly face" and "the slob."

Opposite: Newspaper article about Massimo Periale's horse, "Pushed a Balky Horse," from The Morning Call, Paterson, New Jersey, June 13, 1907.

[La putana con la culla grande]—[The whore with the fat ass]

secondi e contorni

Secondi are meat, poultry and seafood dishes. They are accompanied by contorni, a vegetable course, which is served separately, so as not to mix flavors. Contorni can be cooked or raw, like insalata.

Gertrude, an amazing cook, would gather us all together and feed us delicious family delicacies and cuisine that I always thought were Italian. As an adult I have learned that the concentration of black olives, eggplant and olive oil in most of her recipes was specifically Sicilian. One her favorite recipes, which I still love to prepare is eggplant parmigiana.

gertrude's eggplant parmigiana

2 to 3 large eggplants, cut into slices

3 cups tomato sauce

2 cups mozzarella cheese, sliced thinly

Extra virgin olive oil

Preheat oven to 350°F.

Salt the eggplant slices and layer them in paper towels to absorb any bitter juices. After about thirty minutes pat them dry and sauté the eggplant slices in olive oil. Place on paper towels to absorb excess oil [Gertrude never breaded her eggplant]. When all the eggplant slices are ready, place them on the bottom of a baking dish. Spoon tomato sauce on top of eggplant. Add a layer of mozzarella cheese.

Continue layering in this manner until all ingredients are used. Sprinkle Parmesan cheese on top and bake uncovered for half an hour or until the cheese on top layer has melted.

Variations: 1 cup ricotta cheese, 2 cups cooked ground meat can be used as additional/alternate layers.

Opposite, above and below: Gertrude and family, on the roof of 14th Street, New York, New York, c. 1935 [see page 140 for detailed caption].

Gertrude didn't write down her recipes, but I have some notes. John Angelo loved her southern Italian cooking and this version of bra-ciole she made even more hearty by incorporating ground beef into the stuffing—typically the stuffing consists of parmesan and bread crumbs, or even a slice of prosciutto.

gertrude's braciole

2 pounds. beef steak or veal, sliced and pounded 1/4 inch thick and cut into 4-6 pieces + 1/4 cup cooked ground beef

2 tablespoons minced sweet pepper

2 tablespoons grated cheese [Parmesan or Romano]

3 tablespoons minced parsley

2 cloves garlic

Black pepper, to taste

1/4 cup extra virgin olive oil

3 cups tomato sauce

Spread the meat flat. Mix remaining ingredients, except oil and tomato sauce. Put a bit of the stuffing in the center of each piece and roll up and tie tightly with string at both ends and in the center. Heat oil in a large skillet and sauté rolled meat until well browned on all sides. Add tomato sauce, cover, and simmer slowly for 2 hours or until meat is tender. Clip strings and serve in tomato sauce with pasta, polenta or rice.

Opposite: Periales and Cerchios at Massimo Periale's farm in Cassville, New Jersey, c. 1925 [see page 140 for detailed caption].

[Braciole] - literally, slice of meat roasted over coals.

Gertrude would serve vegetables like zucchini in a light tomato sauce with pasta or a main meat course. Another vegetable-based specialty was her artichoke pie, which could be served at lunch or dinner with a salad or soup.

gertrude's artichoke pie

Pie crust [fresh or frozen] for covered 9" pie

3 tablespoons olive oil

3 cloves garlic

2 9-oz. packages of frozen artichoke hearts [or canned will do]

4 eggs

1/2 cup grated Parmesan cheese

8 oz. mozzarella, cut into small pieces

Preheat oven to 450°F. Heat oil and sauté garlic. Add artichokes and brown quickly over high heat. Spoon into layers in pie shell. Beat together eggs and grated cheese, pour into pie shell. Sprinkle mozzarella. Top with second pie crust, cutting vents. Bake 15 minutes at 450°, lower heat to 350° and bake 30 minutes or until golden brown.

Opposite: In Sea Girt, New Jersey, c. 1968. Above: Elizabeth Anne Periale and Joseph Francis Periale. Below: Gertrude and Elizabeth Anne Periale.

My cousin Lisa Periale shared a great contorno recipe from our Aunt Paula Periale Gerstenberger, Gertrude's daughter. These delicious stuffed mushroms are the perfect side dish [or could even be part of a hot antipasti].

mushrooms paula

1/4 teaspoon garlic powder [or minced garlic]

2 tablespoons dried parsley [or fresh, chopped fine]

1/4 cup grated swiss cheese [mozzarella would work, too]

1/2 cup bread crumbs

2 tablespoons minced onion

1/4 cup dry sherry, Lemon juice

3 tablespoons butter

1 pint of fresh medium-sized mushrooms

Clean and de-stem mushrooms. Chop stems, add lemon juice and sauté in butter. Add grated cheese and bread crumbs. Mix with parsley, garlic powder and onion. Remove mixture from heat, add sherry and toss. Stuff into mushroom caps. Bake 10-15 minutes at 375°F.

insalata

Gertrude always served a green salad to accompany the meal, marinated in her custom oil and vinegar dressing, which was heavy on the black pepper. She would also incorporate any remaining liquid from the condite jar into the dressing. Delicious!

Opposite: Gertrude studio portrait, c. 1909.

dolci

Sorbetto or gelato can be palate-cleansing. Dessert options may include zeppole, cannoli, tiramisu, cake, cookies, or pie.

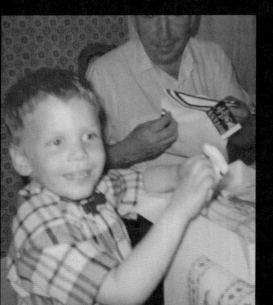

Dessert was mostly served at special occasions, not an every night thing in my family. At Christmastime my uncle John Massimo Periale would always bring a *pannetone* [literally "large cake"] and we would always have *amaretti* [almond cookies] and *torrone* [nougat candy]. Gertrude leaned toward sorbetto, usually served in her fancy candy-colored dessert dishes.

When I think of my grandmother's cooking, I think that Gertrude wasn't much for dessert. If we wanted something sweet her usual response would be, "Eat a piece of fruit." But as I look back I realize that she did make some memorable sweets. Her mincemeat pie was amazing. My brother John James Periale reminded me that she made us cheese cake, but didn't like how much the ingredients cost, so it was a rare treat. She would frequently have Stella D'oro biscotti or cookies with coffee. Those weren't the greatest treats for a kid, as they were a bit dry, like not-too-sweet jawbreakers—they didn't dissolve in milk as easily as they did in Gertrude's coffee. I did like the sesame seed ones, which I've come to learn are originally from Palermo and called *biscotti regina* [queen's biscuits].

Opposite: John James Periale's fourth birthday. CW: With Gertrude, Elizabeth Anne Periale and Joseph Francis Periale, Sea Girt, New Jersey, 1968.

biscotti regina

sicilian sesame seed cookies

2 and 1/2 cups all-purpose flour

1/2 cup sugar

1 teaspoon baking soda

8 tablespoons [room temperature] butter

2 egg yolks

2 and 1/2 tablespoons milk [or you could use the egg whites, adding 3 tablespoons of water]

1 tsp. lemon or orange zest—depending on which flavor you prefer, or fruit you have on hand [Optional addition to dough: 1 tablespoon Anisette, for a licorice flavor]

3/4 cup raw sesame seeds, + more as needed

Combine the dry ingredients first—flour, sugar and baking soda. Add all the other ingredients and mix together until you can form a ball. Wrap the dough in plastic and refrigerate an hour. Preheat oven to 400°F. If you prefer the sesame seeds to be crunchy, toast them in a skillet until they are golden brown in color. Place on a plate. Form thumb-sized biscuits. Dip each one in milk [or egg white mixture] and roll in sesame seeds. Place cookies on a baking sheet lined with parchment paper. Bake for around 10 minutes, or until golden brown. Recipe makes about 3 dozen cookies.

Opposite: Gertrude and family, c. 1969 [see page 143 for detailed caption].

amaretti

2 and 1/2 cups of almond flour

1 and 1/4 cups of finely granulted sugar

3 egg whites

1/2 teaspoon of vanilla extract

1 teaspoon of almond extract

Extra sugar for dusting

In a large mixing bowl, combine the almond flour, sugar, and salt. Place in a food processor and add vanilla and almond extract and mix for a few seconds. Add the egg whites, one at a time, and continue to process until the dough is smooth.

Place small drops of dough onto a baking sheet lined with parchment paper and sprinkle with sugar. Bake at 300°F for 24-30 minutes, or until golden brown.

Cool completely before serving. The amaretti will be slightly chewy at first, but they will become crispier after a few days. Store in a cool, dry place.

Adapted from simply recipes - https://www.simplyrecipes.com/recipes/amaretti_cookies/

Opposite: Gertrude with Elizabeth Anne Periale [and Twinkle], Sea Girt, New Jersey, September 1969.

My uncle John Massimo loved to pass on jokes and stories that he heard from his relatives over the years. One of his favorite "characters" was his Aunt Ernie, his father John Angelo's sister, who was full of mischief as a kid. A kindred spirit.

When John Angelo was just a baby his older sister Ernie was told to take him out for a walk. She set him in the pram and off they went. Walking her baby brother's carriage at first seemed a chore, but Ernie, who was always on the lookout for a game, soon got an idea of how to make it more fun. She pushed him to the top of the hill near where they lived in Paterson, New Jersey. She gave the carriage a little push and hopped in behind John Angelo as it started to roll down the hill. For a few moments it was a fun rollercoaster ride, but when they got to the bottom of the hill the pram hit a rock and went over. Ernie went out one side of the carriage and the baby went out the other, flying into a horse trough. Luckily neither was harmed, but John Angelo was sopping wet. Ernie walked him around for hours, waiting for him to dry off.

When she finally brought him home, Paolina asked her where they had been all afternoon.

"Out for a walk," she said proudly.

Paolina took this answer in quietly and responded, "Ernie, then could you answer one question—why are the baby's clothes on backwards?"

Opposite: Gertrude and John James Periale, Spring Lake, New Jersey, c. 1976.

Torrone was a staple treat at Chrismastime with my family, either giving or receiving the delicious confectionary. Gertrude loved it, but as far as I know never made it herself, so I have put together a recipe to make my own.

torrone

3 and 1/3 cups raw nuts [almonds, pistachios, hazelnuts, or a combination of all three]

2 and 1/4 cups + 1 tablespoon granulated sugar

1 and 1/2 cups honey

3 egg whites

1 pinch salt

1/4 teaspoon vanilla extract

Edible rice paper

Preheat the oven to 350°F. Spread out the nuts in a single layer on a sheet pan and place in the oven until they are toasted slightly. Remove from the oven and let cool.

Butter the sides of an 8-inch by 12-inch baking tray Line the bottom with a sheet of edible rice paper. Put honey and sugar in a sturdy saucepan, stirring constantly over medium heat until completely dissolved and smooth and silky in texture. Remove from heat.

Opposite: Gertrude at Christmas, Waretown, New Jersey, c. 1978. Above: with Joseph Francis Periale. Below: Gertrude opens presents.

Whisk the egg whites with a pinch of salt until they form soft peaks. Place pan with sugar and honey back on low heat and gradually add the egg white mixture. Continue cooking over low heat, stirring constantly. Whisk in vanilla and add nuts to the mixture, stirring to incorporate evenly. The mixture should be somewhat stiff in texture. Pour into the baking tray and spread out as evenly as possible.

Place second sheet of edible rice paper on top. You can place a piece of parchment paper and use a rolling pin to flatten. Allow the torrone to set overnight or until cool and ready to cut.

Above: Gertrude and family, c. 1935. [see page 143 for detailed caption].

Gertrude did make coffee cake—a pecan danish ring. It must have been one of my father Joseph Francis's favorites, as she made it quite often. The cake was usually served as a special sweet with weekend breakfast, not as an evening dessert.

gertrude's coffee cake

Dough:

2 cups of all-purpose flour

1 and 1/2 tablespoons sugar

1/2 teaspoon salt

1/2 cup of cold butter

1/2 cup of milk [scald, then cool]

1 egg, separated

1 package active dry yeast [2 and 1/4 teaspoons]

1/4 cup of warm water

Pecan Filling:

3/4 cup pecans

1/2 cup brown sugar

1/4 cup butter

1 tablespoon flour

Glaze:

1 and 1/4 cups powdered sugar

1 tablespoon + 1 teaspoon water

1 teaspoon vanilla

Combine flour, sugar and salt, cutting butter into mixture. Stir egg yolk into cool milk, add to dry ingredients mixture. Add yeast to warm water and let stand a few minutes and then add to flour mixture, mixing thoroughly. Dough will be very soft. Cover bowl tightly and chill for at least 2 hours, or preferably, overnight in refrigerator. Divide dough into 2 parts. Roll out one part of dough into 6 x 18 inch rectangle as thin as possible. Spread filling down middle of the dough. Fold over one side, then the other. Pinch to close the fold. Slide onto greased baking sheet and form into an oval. Dough will release some filling out of seams, which is OK. Beat egg white until frothy. Brush dough with egg glaze.

Cover and let rise in warm place for 45 minutes or until double in size. Bake at 350°F for 15-20 minutes until golden brown. Sprinkle immediately with nuts and drizzle with glaze when cool. Recipe makes two pecan danish rings.

Gertrude's crumb coffee cake was always a special treat. The only clue I have to its making is a scribbled ingredients list she tucked in her cookbook. But that hasn't stopped me from trying to cobble together a recipe.

gertrude's crumb coffee cake

cake:

2 tablespoons vegetable oil

4 cups all-purpose flour

1/2 cup granulated sugar

2 and 1/2 teaspoons baking powder

1/2 teaspoon salt

1 large egg

1/2 cup milk

2 teaspoons pure vanilla extract

crumb topping:

1 cup light-brown sugar, firmly packed

1 and 1/2 teaspoons ground cinnamon

1 cup unsalted butter, melted and cooled

Powdered sugar, for dusting

Opposite: Gertrude's crumb coffee cake was legendary.

Preheat oven to 325°F. Lightly brush a 9x13-inch baking pan with cooking oil.

In a medium bowl, sift together 1 and 1/2 cups flour, granulated sugar, baking powder, and salt. In a second bowl, whisk together the egg, milk, vegetable oil and vanilla. Fold dry ingredients into egg mixture and spread batter evenly into baking pan.

In a medium bowl, combine remaining 2 and 1/2 cups flour, brown sugar, and cinnamon. Pour melted butter over flour mixture, stirring until large crumbs form. Top batter evenly with crumb topping. Bake for 35 to 40 minutes or until the cake tests done. Dust with powdered sugar after cooling.

Above: John James Periale at the kitchen table, Spring Lake Heights, New Jersey, c. 1966.

Lisa shared her version of Gertrude's Italian Coffee Cake:

"I never had a recipe for this. Grandma would say to just watch her. She told me: 'First, you make a brioche.'

I said, 'What's a brioche?'

She told me that it is an 'egg-y, cake-y yeast bread that has an egg for each cup of flour you use.' I have chosen different brioche recipes over the years, but I stick to that balance of eggs and flour. Some recipes call for making a 'sponge' to add to the yeast of the flour mixture. But Grandma didn't do this, so neither do I."

gertrude's italian coffee cake

brioche:

1 tablespoon active dry yeast [1 packet is fine]

1/3 cup warm water

3 and 1/2 cups flour

1 tablespoon sugar

4 eggs [reserve 1 egg white for use later]

3/4 cup butter, softened

In a small bowl, dissolve yeast in warm water. Let stand until creamy, about 10 minutes. You can put 1/4–1/2 teaspoon of honey in the mix if you want to make sure it gets active. Separate the white of one of the eggs. You will use later to brush the coffee cake before it goes in the oven. In a large bowl, stir together the flour and sugar. Make a well in center of the bowl and mix in the butter, eggs and yeast mixture.

Beat well until the dough has pulled together, then turn it out onto a well floured surface and knead until smooth and uniform. Grease a large bowl with olive oil. Put the dough in to rise. Cover with wax paper [a little olive oil on the surface right above the dough is helpful], then cover with a kitchen towel. Let it sit in a warm place for a few hours. If the house is chilly, turn on the oven for a while, then turn it off, and then place the bowl on the slightly warm stovetop.

When the dough has risen [sometimes it will double, sometimes it doesn't quite get there], punch it down, knead it briefly, and then turn out onto a large cookie sheet covered in foil. I usually put a sheen of olive oil on the foil before I put on the dough. Spread out the dough to cover or nearly cover the pan. Let it rise in the pan while you make the filling and preheat the oven to 375°F.

filling:

1/2 cup of butter

2 cups of chopped walnuts

1 cup of raisins or black currants

2 teaspoons of cinnamon

1/4–1/2 cup brown sugar to taste

1/2 cup orange juice

Opposite: Little Silver, New Jersey, c. 1978. Above: Camera-shy Gertrude with granddaughters Lisa Periale and Elizabeth Anne Periale, . Below: Lisa Periale.

Melt the butter in a sauce pan over low heat. Slowly add the rest of the ingredients, except the orange juice. Once everything is well mixed, gradually add a little orange juice until mixture is moist, but not too liquid—otherwise it will seep out of the coffee cake as it bakes. Take the filling off the burner and let it cool a little.

Now you have a choice. A simple approach is to put the filling over just one half of the dough, with more in the center than the edge, and then fold the other half of dough over to cover the rest. This is what Gertrude traditionally did. Sometimes I cover all of the dough, roll it up like a cylinder, form it into a circular ring, make some cuts along the top two thirds, every two inches or so, then pull it apart a bit to expose the filling.

No matter what design you use, brush the whole thing liberally with the reserved egg white before you bake it. It should bake for 25–30 minutes, but check at 20 minutes. Stick a thin knife in the doughiest section to see if it comes out clean. Once it does and the dough is nicely browned, remove from oven and let cool.

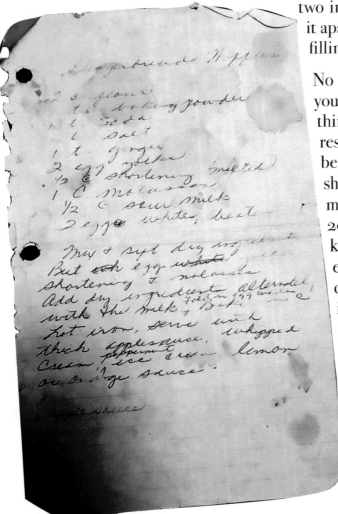

Lisa also shared a delicious waffle recipe that Gertrude probably adapted from a magazine recipe.

gingerbread waffles

2 cups flour

1 teaspoon baking powder

1/2 teaspoon baking soda

1 teaspoon salt

1 teaspoon ginger

2 egg yolks

1/2 cup shortening [melted]

1 cup molasses

1/2 cup sour milk

2 egg whites, beaten

Mix and sift dry ingredients. Beat together egg yolks, shortening and molasses. Add dry ingredients, alternating with the milk. Fold in egg whites. Bake in hot waffle iron. Serve with thick applesauce, whipped cream, peppermint ice cream, lemon or orange sauce.

Opposite:Gertrude's gingerbread waffles recipe in her handwriting.

Another Christmastime staple in an Italian or Italian-American household is panettone. Sadly, I don't think she was still making this when I was a kid, but here is her recipe.

gertrude's panettone

Dose [Amounts]

Libre [Pounds]

Onzi [Ounce. Not a direct translation, maybe Sicilian dialect—in Italian, "oncia"]

Farina [Flour]—3 libre

Lievito di birra [Brewer's yeast]—1 onzi

Zucchero [Sugar]—6 onzi

Burro [Butter]—6 onzi

Uova intieri [Whole egg]—6

Centro e uva passa [Center and raisins]—8 onzi

Prima lievatura / ore [First rising/hours]—4 ore

Seconda . . . [Second rising/hours]—2 ore

Forno non troppo caldo [Oven not too hot]

Opposite: Gertrude's panettone ingredients list, in Italian.

Panettone di Milano
Dose

	Libre	onzi
Farina	3	
lievito di birra		1
zucchero ✓		6
Burro ✓		6
uova intieri	N	6
Cetro e uva passa		8

Prima lievatura ore 4
Seconda " ... ore 2
forno non troppo Caldo

caffe e digestivo

Strong espresso without any milk or sugar, or cappucino at the end of the meal, as well as tea or a liquer is always welcome.

After Paolina died in 1926, the family wondered what they were going to do with Massimo. He didn't want to go live with anyone in the family, he wanted to live on his own. He bought a farm in South Jersey, near Fort Dix with 3 acres of arable land and 23 acres of woods. He decided he was going to raise chickens and got about 2,000. He was in his seventies at the time.

One day one of his old *paisanos* from northern Italy came by, "You know, *Celin* [his nickname for Massimo], with all this land and those woods near the fort, you could make some nice money making whiskey."

It didn't take long for Massimo to decide. "Let's go!"

So the two old pals started making booze. This was taking place during prohibition, of course.

John Angelo, who at this time was living with his family in the Bronx, drove to New Jersey one day to check on his father and see how he was doing without Paolina. They spent the day together. John Angelo came back to New York and told Gertrude, "You know, something's going on down there. I can't quite put my finger on it. But there are chickens all over the place. In the house. In the yard. He's got a big wine press. It's a mess, there's no order anywhere. And there's this awful smell coming from the woods."

About a month or so after his visit John Angelo got a call from one of Massimo's neighbors, a farmer who lived down the road, "Mr. Periale—you better come down here right away, your dad's in trouble."

John Angelo got into his Flint and again drove to New Jersey. He looked all over the farm, but there was no sign of Massimo. He made some calls and finally got hold of the family's resident problem-solver, his sister Della. She told him, "Yes he's here and we've

Opposite: Joseph Francis Periale and Mary Elizabeth Winship Periale. Above: At an airport, c. 1961. Below: Cafe Madrid, New York, New York, c. 1965.

got problems. You better come up."

So John Angelo got back in his car and headed up to Ridgewood in North Jersey. Della had quite a story to tell. That morning Massimo was at the farm as his buddy came chugging down the road in his car and said, "Get in, they're 15 minutes behind me."

He was referring to the revenue agents. They chased the two old geezers all the way from South Jersey up to Ridgewood. With Della's husband Dr. David "Daoud" Himadi's pull, they tried to keep Massimo out of jail by pleading compassion. They appealed to the judge, citing Massimo's age and recent loss of his wife. The judge called him up to the bench and started to lecture him. Massimo interrupted and turned to Della, "What's he talking about?"

Della whispered, "You're not supposed to make whiskey."

Massimo became angry, "Nobody tells me not to make whiskey. If I wanna make whiskey, I make whiskey!"

Della, in a louder tone, "Shut up! Take your hat off!"

Massimo, stubbornly, "But I make whiskey!"

Della, loudly, "Shut up!"

He almost got thrown in jail. John Angelo, who had studied law, helped negotiate. Della paid the fine. The still was confiscated. The agents discovered a big hole in the fence between his property and Fort Dix. He had been selling bootleg whiskey through the fence to the GI's!

D'Ippolito/Periale

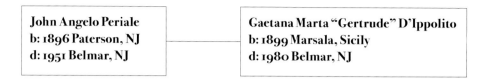

John Angelo Periale	Gaetana Marta "Gertrude" D'Ippolito
b: 1896 Paterson, NJ	b: 1899 Marsala, Sicily
d: 1951 Belmar, NJ	d: 1980 Belmar, NJ

John Massimo Periale
b: 1921 New York, NY
d: 1998 Orlando, FL

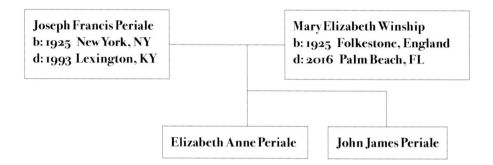

Joseph Francis Periale	Mary Elizabeth Winship
b: 1925 New York, NY	b: 1925 Folkestone, England
d: 1993 Lexington, KY	d: 2016 Palm Beach, FL

Elizabeth Anne Periale	John James Periale

Paula Periale
b: 1927 Queens, NY

James Gabriel Periale
b: 1932 New York, NY

coffee and liquers

Sometimes in the afternoon Gertrude would take a spoonful of ground coffee [Medaglia D'Oro] and chew the grounds. She would have a glass of Port when she had *agita* or a tooth ache. Red wine was omnipresent. And white, at dessert time. In the 1970s the Italian-named Gallo wines were all the rage, as were wine-making kits. My parents managed to create a pretty good vinegar . . .

After-dinner liquers such as Amaretto [almond flavored] and Galliano [anise and vanilla flavored] would be served. Sometimes Gertrude would sip a little Marsala, the wine from her birthplace in Sicily. Every once in a while she'd add a little Marsala to her coffee cup. At one occasion that I remember we had vanilla ice cream with Galliano poured on top—simply delicious. Gertrude always made coffee for the adults for after dinner. Kids rarely found anything to drink at her house besides milk or the occasional ginger ale. I don't remember anyone just drinking water in those days unless they came in from being outside for a long time and had to rehydrate. On special occasions a digestive alcoholic drink, such as limoncello or grappa, might be served.

Buon appetito!

Opposite: John James Periale serves "tea" to Elizabeth Anne Periale, Sea Girt, New Jersey, c. 1968.

[Agita]—Italian-American slang meaning heartburn, upset stomach or general upset. It is derived from the Italian word [agitare]—to agitate.

acknowledgments

Growing up with a Sicilian grandmother I learned to appreciate great food. It was part of life—at least my life. I also learned at a very early age how lucky I was when many friends thought a spaghetti dinner was opening a can of Spaghetti-Os. If we were at Grandma's for dinner she did all the cooking—I could "watch and learn." If she was at our house for dinner she was invariably in the kitchen with my mother, not directing, but assisting. I can't recall ever eating out at a restaurant with Grandma. If we were going out to dinner for some special ocassion she would decline the invitation, but suggest we stop by afterwards for coffee and dessert.

Probably the most frequent meal we had with Grandma was spaghetti and meatballs. Or maybe she just always had spaghetti as part of the meal, whether it was a fancy braciole or eggplant parmesan.

I am grateful to my family for sharing their memories and recipes for this cookbook/storybook. Great meals are always made better by sharing them with your loved ones.

Abbondanza!

Opposite: Triumvirate: L-R: Barbara Rose Periale, Gertrude and Elizabeth Anne Periale, Little Silver, New Jersey, c. 1978.

[Abbondanza]—Literal meaning is abundance, plenty, but is frequently used as a wish for plenty, celebration.

1—Nicola Cerchio	13—Pauline Angelicola
2—Edward Coda	14—Paola Cerchio Periale
3—Rose Periale Coda	15—Secondo "Parin" Cerchio
4—"Chook" Gillia	16—Erminia Bianchi Cerchio
5—Margaret Periale	17—Joe Coda
6—Ernie Periale Gillia	18—Elena Cerchio
7—Charlie Cerchio	21—Nicholas Cerchio, Jr.
8—Della Periale	24—Alfred Louis Cerchio
9—Clelia Cerchio	25—Vincent Angelicola
10—Frank Periale*	27—Lola Cerchio
11—Massimo Periale	28—John Angelo Periale
12—Lena Periale Angelicola	*best guess

• •

In 1911 the Periales were:

Massimo—53

Paola—48

Lena—27, [Husband Daniel Angelicola—34, Children Vincent—8, Adelaide—5, Carlo—4, Gemma—3, Pauline—1]

Rose—25 [Husband Joseph Coda—32, Children Lillian—3, Edward—2]

Ernie—24, [Husband Chook—37, Children Kenneth—5, Paul—2]

Della—21

Frank—20

John Angelo—15

Margaret—13

Opposite, above: At Massimo Periale's house, Lodi, NJ, 1911, after the Paterson, New Jersey fire. Below: Picture key.

about the author

gertrude's table

is an original work. inspired by family gatherings, great food, and the stories that were told again and again, a little different with each telling.

elizabeth periale

is an artist and writer. She graduated from Parsons School of Design in New York with a concentration in painting. She hails from Neptune, New Jersey and lives in West Palm Beach, Florida with her daughter. She has worked as a graphic designer and artist in New York, Washington, D.C., and Florida. Elizabeth debuted her blog, xoxoxo e, in 2008. She has contributed articles and reviews to the Smithsonian Libraries, Yahoo! News, Cinema Sentries, BlogHer, Cannonball Read, and Blogcritics. She is the illustrator and author of the novels *Unfinished: A Graphic Novel of Marilyn Monroe* [2017] and *Jason + Medea* [2020], and the graphic novels *Alice and Johnny and Sex and Violence . . . and Bob* [2018] and *Walk At Night* [2018].

Above: Elizabeth Anne Periale and Mary Elizabeth Winship Periale at the celebration of Elizabeth Anne Periale's 4th birthday, Gotham Hotel, New York, New York, September 1966.

and dissolve yeast
1/4 Cup luke warm water
Cream sugar & butter
Beat eggs and add
then add 3 cups
sifted flour & let
raise

only when water comes to a
Let the Lobster boil
only 5 minute
and then take out
and prepare

All photos from the collection of Elizabeth Anne Periale, unless otherwise noted.

Cover, title page and 147—Gertrude D'Ippolito in Paterson, New Jersey, c. 1920.

3—Gaetana Marta "Gertrude" D'Ippolito in communion dress, New York, c. 1906. Photography studio—S. Vitali, 88-90 Catherine St., New York.

4—New York World's Fair, Queens, New York, c.1939. L-R: Joseph Francis Periale, James Gabriel Periale, Paula Periale, Gertrude.

7—Gertrude and Elizabeth Anne Periale, Spring Lake Heights, New Jersey, c. 1963.

9—Above: Frank D'Ippolito was a cook like his father, Don Peppino. In 1918 he was a cook at the Brick Hotel in Spring Lake, New Jersey. Below: Frank admires a car . . . John Angelo Periale's Franklin, with Ernie Periale Gillia behind the wheel, at Massimo Periale's Cassville, New Jersey farm, c. 1925.

Opposite: One of Gertrude's recipes for a lobster dish found tucked in her cookbook. Above: Joseph Francis Periale with a young customer, Belmar, New Jersey, c. 1945.

10–Above: Gertrude at her dining table. L-R: Gertrude, Margaret Periale D'Ippolito, Joseph Francis Periale, July 8, 1934. Below: Secundo "Parin' Cerchio and his family in North Beach, Long Island, July 12, 1910. L-R: Charles A Cerchio [17], Secundo Cerchio [age 75], Margaret Periale [12] with Kenneth Gillia [4] on lap, Ernesta "Ernie" Periale Gillia [23], Della Periale [20], Clelia Cerchio [14], Paola Cerchio Periale [46], and Lola Cerchio [12] in front on hubcap [courtesy of Louis Cerchio].

A funny story about Parin and his wife Carolina Livorno that Gertrude liked to tell: Carolina was very quiet and sweet-natured and Parin loved to tease her. One cold morning they were looking out of the window at their chickens scratching in the dirt and Carolina, a timid soul, was worried that the chickens would freeze during the cold winter months. "How will we keep the chickens warm?" she asked her husband. Parin answered, "You know what you should do, you should knit them booties." She took him at his word. "Oh, naturalmente!" And she did.

Above: Mary Elizabeth Winship Periale visiting Della Periale Himadi while on honeymoon with Joseph Francis Periale, St. Augustine, Florida, November, 1961. Opposite: Gertrude [in outfit with black and white stripes] with her Giddings co-workers, Bryant Park, New York , c. 1934 [see page 144 for detailed caption].

1 1/2 cup sugar

2 1/2 flour

5 — eggs

2 1/2 teaspoonful
B. Powder

1/2 cup butter
about 1/4 lb. butter

1/2 cup of milk

Rind of a lemon

12—Above: 1905 New York State Census [detail]. Below: 1910 United States Census [detail].

13—D'Ippolito family tree.

15—Watercolor by James Gabriel D'Ippolito, c. 1916 [signed J. J. D'Ippolito].

17—Cabinet card of Gertrude's older sisters Mary D'Ippolito and Filomena "Fanny" D'Ippolito with their mother Giovannina Quartuccio D'Ippolito [seated], c. 1905 [scrawled on the back in pencil: 261 Elizabeth, I floor, back].

19—Above: Gertrude relaxes with the evening paper. 14th Street, New York, c. 1926. Below: Gertrude with lilacs in Manasquan, New Jersey, c. 1970. [courtesy of Susan Periale McCarthy]

20—Wedding photo of Gertrude's sister Mary D'Ippolito and Joseph Battaglia, c. 1914. [Photography studio—S. Vitali, 2 Monroe St., New York].

Opposite: This looks to be a list to create a lemon cake of some sort, in Gertrude's handwriting [courtesy of Pamela McCorkle Periale]. Above: Coffee break: Gertrude [seated, second from right] with garment district coworkers, c. 1934.

22—Location map of downtown New York, noting where the D'Ippolitos lived. Photos of 261 Elizabeth Street, the site of Don Peppino's restaurant, taken in 1999 and 2019. In 1910 Don Peppino owned the restaurant and the family lived a few blocks away at 324 Bowery. By 1915 they had all moved "uptown" to 93 3rd Avenue and 13th Street, but Don Peppino was no longer in the restaurant business. By 1920 they were living at 349 East 14th Street, where they lived until 1933, when Don Peppino died. [see photos od 14th Street on page 32].

23—Wedding photo of Gertrude's sister Filomena "Fanny" D'Ippolito, who married Frank Battaglia, 1913. [Photography studio—Spiess Studio, 54 Second Av., New York. Written on back: Mr. D'Ippolito, 349 E. 14th St., First Floor, Battalla].

24—Family memento: travel brochure for Taormina, Sicily.

26— On an outing, Paterson, New Jersey, c. 1920. Above: Albert D'Ippolito, Margaret Periale, Gertrude and John Angelo Periale. Below: Gertrude and John Angelo Periale.

28—Left: Wedding photo of Margaret Periale and Albert D'Ippolito. Right: Gertrude and John Angelo Periale, c. 1920 [courtesy of John James Periale].

29—Don Peppino's parlor, 14th Street, New York, c. 1923. L-R: Unknown relative, John Massimo Periale and Gertrude, reflected in mirror.

30— Don Peppino's parlor, 14th Street, New York, c. 1923. Above: Gertrude and John Massimo Periale. Below: John Massimo Periale.

32—349 East 14th Street, photographed in the mid-1970s [above] and in 2019 [inset]. Don Peppino's office faced the street, with the family living in rooms towards the back of the building. The D'Ippolitos and Periales lived on two floors. The building originally had a stoop and the ground floor was a store that sold prosthetics and other medical supplies. Top photo: Mary Elizabeth Winship Periale and Elizabeth Anne Periale standing in front of Allen's Bar.

33—Double portrait of Gertrude, c. 1950.

Opposite, above: Gertrude in Brooklyn, New York, c. 1958. L-R: Albert D'Ippolito, Margaret Periale D'Ippolito, Gertrude, Ernie Periale Gillia and Della Periale Himadi. Below: Gertrude with family in Spring Lake Heights, New Jersey, c. 1966 [see page 144 for detailed caption].

34—Above: John Angelo Periale and Gertrude on Broadway, New York, c. 1930. Below: Joseph D'Ippolito, AKA Don Peppino, and his grandchildren, 14th Street, New York, c. 1930. L-R:Joe D'Ippolito, Johanna D'Ippolito, Palma Battaglia, John Massimo Periale, Joseph D'Ippolito [Don Peppino, seated], Joseph Francis Periale, Paula Periale.

Acccording to John Massimo: "Don Peppino was the D'Ippolito/Periale pater familias. If anyone needed money, Don Peppino would pull out his roll of bills [his "wad," as Joseph Francis Periale would call it], and help them out. He helped everyone out.

36—Gertrude's sfincioni shopping list [*courtesy Pamela McCorkle Periale*].
I have another recipe/list in which she has directions for chopping onions "about the size of a horse's teeth." I miss Grandma.

38—My notes for Gertrude's sfincioni recipe.

I don't remember ever eating out at a restaurant with my grandmother Gertrude. She may have been a chef's daughter, but she preferred to eat at home—and do all the cooking.

39—Gertrude entered her Sicilian family delicacy into the Pillsbury Baking contest, in 1962, but called it "Antipasto Tasty Loaf." I guess she thought that might be a less confusing name than Sfincioni. She didn't win, sadly. Philistines. [*courtesy of Susan Periale McCarthy*].

41—Above: Due fratelli—Unknown relatives from Palermo, Sicily, [Don Peppino and his brother Andrea?] Below: Don Peppino [?].

43—Above: Telling stories, Little Silver, New Jersey, July 25, 1979. L-R: James Gabriel Periale, Mary Elizabeth Winship Periale, Elizabeth Anne Periale, Gertrude, John Massimo Periale, Albert D'Ippolito, Marie Peze Morris. Below: Triumvirate- L-R: Albert D'Ippolito, Joseph Francis Periale and John Massimo Periale at Gertrude's 80th birthday celebration, Little Silver, New Jersey, July 25, 1979.

45—Gertrude and family. L-R: Joe D'Ippolito, Paula Periale, Gertrude, Joseph Francis Periale and James Gabriel Periale [in front], McGraw Avenue, Bronx, New York, c. 1937.

46—John Massimo Periale, c. 1931.

Opposite, above: Gertrude and John Massimo Periale, 14th Street, New York, New York, c. 1923. Below: Gertrude and Elizabeth Anne Periale, Spring Lake Heights, New Jersey, Easter 1963.

48—L-R: Rose Anzalone Periale, Gertrude, James Gabriel Periale, Joseph Francis Periale and Giovannina Quartuccio D'Ippolito [the only photo I have of her], Belmar, N.J., c. 1942.

51—Dinner at Gertrude's, Spring Lake, New Jersey, c. 1979. Above, L-R: John Massimo Periale, Gertrude, Barbara Rose Periale. Below: James Gabriel Periale and John Massimo Periale.

53—John Massimo Periale and Rose Anzalone Periale, c. 1942.

54—Gertrude at the piano, with Joseph "Giuseppe" D'Ippolito, AKA Don Peppino, looking on, New York, New York, c. 1919.

57—Gertrude's opera libretto of "Lakme," by Léo Delibes.

58—Elizabeth Anne Periale with Gertrude, Sea Girt, New Jersey, c. 1968.

63—Periale ladies at the beach, c. 1921. L-R: Della Periale Himadi, Paola Cerchio Periale, Margaret Periale D'Ippolito and Ernie Periale Gillia.

65—James Gabriel Periale, Bronx, New York, c. 1938.

66—John Angelo Periale, c. 1916.

67—John Angelo Periale and Gertrude, c.1943.

68—Periales and Cerchios in Lodi, New Jersey, c. 1925. L-R: David Himadi, Gertrude, Margaret Periale D'Ippolito holding Johanna D'Ippolito, John Angelo Periale holding Joseph Francis Periale, Ernie Periale Gillia.

69—Periale family tree.

Above: Gertrude studio portrait [detail], c. 1909. Opposite: I Cugini, Little Silver, New Jersey, c. 1980 [see page 144 for detailed caption].

71—Gertrude's cookbook, held together by ribbon, contained a few sheets with dashed off ingredients that we can piece together like archaeology to recreate her recipes. [*The Century Cook Book, by Mary Ronald, 1901, courtesy of Pamela McCorkle Periale*].

73—Paolina Cerchio Periale visits her brother Nicola Cerchio's family in Wilmington, Delaware, 1915. Back row, L-R: Paolina Cerchio Periale, Della Periale, John Cerchio, Clelia Cerchio, Erminia Bianchi Cerchio. Front row, L-R: Lola Cerchio, Alfred Cerchio, Elena Cerchio, Charlie Cerchio, Nick Cerchio Jr , Nicola Cerchio Sr. [*courtesy of Louis Cerchio*].

74—Paolina Cerchio Periale, c. 1910.

77—1922 Calendar from Periale & Sons French Bakers, 27 East Place, Lodi, New Jersey. [*courtesy of John James Periale*].

79—Paolina Cerchio Periale and her daughters, c. 1910. L-R: Della Periale, Ernie Periale Gillia, Paolina Cerchio Periale.

Above: Periale siblings. L-R: Ernie Periale Gillia, John Angelo Periale and Margaret Periale D'Ippolito, McGraw Avenue, Bronx, New York, c. 1940. Opposite: On the Hudson River Dayline, c. 1923 [see page 146 for more detailed caption].

80—Della Periale Himadi, age 28, with son David Himadi in 1918.

In 2019 I was contacted on Ancestry.com by a genealogist who does a lot of research on Paterson, New Jersey, where his family has lived for many generations. He had recently purchased a collection of photographs on eBay from a Paterson-based family. As he was making digital copies he came across one labeled "Della Himadi." Once we verified that she was the same woman from my family tree he sent me this lovely photo.

82—Newspaper article about Massimo Periale's horse, "Pushed a Balky Horse," from The Morning Call, Paterson, New Jersey, June 13, 1907.

84—Gertrude and family, on the roof of 14th Street, New York, New York, c. 1935. Above: Back row, L-R: Margaret Periale D'Ippolito, [Gertrude's brother] Frank D'Ippolito, Gertrude, John Angelo Periale, Joseph D'Ippolito [Frank and Angelina D'Ippolito's son]. Front row, L-R: Philomena D'Ippolito [Frank and Angelina D'Ippolito's daughter], Joe D'Ippolito and Johanna D'Ippolito [Albert and Margaret D'Ippolito's children], James Gabriel Periale, Paula Periale and Joseph Francis Periale. Below: L-R: Gertrude with brother Frank D'Ippolito and John Angelo Periale with sister Margaret Periale D'Ippolito.

87—Periales and Cerchios at Massimo's farm in Cassville, New Jersey, c. 1925. Above, L-R: Della Periale Himadi with [?],[?],[?], David Himadi with John Massimo Periale, Albert D'Ippolito holding Johanna D'Ippolito, Frank D'Ippolito, Massimo Periale, [?], [?]. Below,: Everyone posing in front of John Angelo Periale's Franklin. He was testing his "Periometer" invention [see page 145]. Back row, L-R: Gertrude, John Angelo Periale holding Joseph Francis Periale, Margaret Periale D'Ippolito holding Johanna D'Ippolito, Frank D'Ippolito, Della Periale Himadi, Dr. Daoud "David" Himadi, Ernie Periale Gillia, [?],[?],[?],[?],[?],[?], Massimo Periale. Front row: David Himadi, [?], John Massimo Periale.

89—In Sea Girt, New Jersey, c. 1968. Above: Elizabeth Anne Periale and Joseph Francis Periale. Below: Gertrude and Elizabeth Anne Periale.

91—Gertrude studio portrait, c. 1909. [*courtesy of Paula Periale Gerstenberger*].

92—John James Periale's fourth birthday. CW: With Gertrude, Elizabeth Anne Periale and Joseph Francis Periale, Sea Girt, New Jersey, 1968.

Opposite: Above:,Periales and D'Ippolitios, c. 1935 [see page 146 for detailed caption]. Below, Gertrude with Elizabeth Anne Periale, Spring Lake Heights, New Jersey, c. 1964.

95—Gertrude and family, in Ridgewood, New Jersey, c. 1969. Standing, L-R: Myra Jean "Petey" Morris Periale, Lisa Periale, Marie Peze Morris, Judith Periale Susan Periale, Mary Elizabeth Winship Periale, Gertrude. Seated, L-R: Somnuk "Som" Jetjirawat, Joseph Francis Periale, Elizabeth Anne Periale, John James Periale.

96—Gertrude with Elizabeth Anne Periale [and Twinkle], Sea Girt, New Jersey, September 1969.

99—Gertrude and John James Periale, Spring Lake, New Jersey, c. 1976.

100—Opposite: Gertrude at Christmas, Waretown, New Jersey, c. 1978. Above: with Joseph Francis Periale. Below: Gertrude opens presents.

102—Gertrude and family. L-R: Paula Periale, Margaret Periale D'Ippolito, Joe D'Ippolito, Gertrude, James Gabriel Periale, Bronx, New York, c. 1935.

104—Gertrude's crumb coffee cake was legendary—another ingredients list in her handwriting.

106— John James at the kitchen table, Spring Lake Heights, New Jersey, c. 1966.

109— Little Silver, New Jersey, c. 1978. Above: Camera-shy Gertrude with grand-daughters Lisa Periale and Elizabeth Anne Periale. Below: Lisa Periale.

110—Gertrude's gingerbread waffles recipe in her handwriting [courtesy of Lisa Periale Martin].

113—Gertrude's panettone ingredients list in Italian, [courtesy of Pamela McCorkle Periale].

114—Joseph Francis Periale and Mary Elizabeth Winship Periale. Above: At an airport, c. 1961. Below: Cafe Madrid, New York, New York, c. 1965.

117—D'Ippolito/Periale family tree.

119—John James Periale serves "tea" to Elizabeth Anne Periale, Sea Girt, New Jersey, c. 1968.

120—Triumvirate: L-R: Barbara Rose Periale, Gertrude and Elizabeth Anne Periale, Little Silver, New Jersey, c. 1978.

122—Above: At Massimo's house, Lodi, New Jersey, 1911, after the Paterson, New Jersey fire. Below: Picture key.

Opposite: Above, Massimo Periale and Paola Cerchio Periale [?]. Below: Massimo Periale [?].

125—Elizabeth Anne Periale and Mary Elizabeth Winship Periale at the celebration of Elizabeth Anne Periale's 4th birthday, Gotham Hotel, New York, New York, September 1966.

126—One of Gertrude's recipes for a lobster dish found tucked in her cookbook. [courtesy of Pamela McCorkle Periale].

127—Joseph Francis Periale with a young customer, Belmar, New Jersey, c. 1945.

128—Mary Elizabeth Winship Periale visiting Della Periale Himadi while on honeymoon with Joseph Francis Periale, St. Augustine, Florida, November 1961.

129—Gertrude [in outfit with black and white stripes] with her Giddings co-workers, Bryant Park, New York, c. 1934. Above: At the Josephine Shaw Lowell Fountain. Below: At the William Cullen Bryant memorial.

130—This looks to be a list to create a lemon cake of some sort, in Gertrude's handwriting [courtesy of Pamela McCorkle Periale].

131—Coffee break at Giddings: Gertrude [seated, second from right] with garment district coworkers, c. 1934.

133—Above: Gertrude in Brooklyn, New York, c. 1958. L-R: Albert D'Ippolito, Margaret Periale D'Ippolito, Gertrude, Ernie Periale Gillia and Della Periale Himadi. Below: Gertrude with family in Spring Lake Heights, New Jersey. CW: Barbara Rose Periale, Rose Anzalone Periale, Gertrude with Elizabeth Anne Periale on lap, Joseph Francis Periale with John James Periale on lap, Mary Elizabeth Winship Periale.

134—Above: Gertrude and John Massimo Periale, 14th Street, New York, New York, c. 1923. Below: Gertrude and Elizabeth Anne Periale, Spring Lake Heights, New Jersey, Easter 1963.

136—Gertrude studio portrait [detail], c. 1909 [*courtesy of Paula Periale Gerstenberger*].

137—I Cugini, Little Silver, New Jersey, c. 1980. CW: Myra Jean "Petey" Morris Periale, Peter Gerstenberger, Mary "Mim" Casciato Gerstenberger, Leigh Gerstenberger, Lisa Periale, Andrew Periale, Susan Periale, Judith Periale, Ann Gerstenberger, Elizabeth Anne Periale.

Opposite: Schematic for John Angelo Periale's patented "Periometer," November 6, 1928.

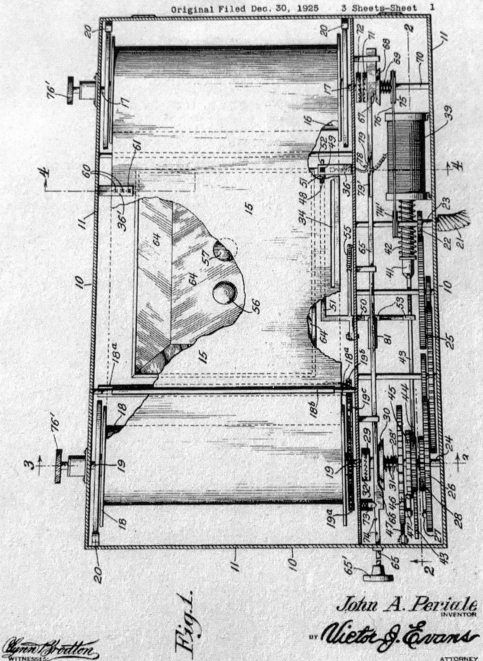

Fig.1.

John A. Periale
INVENTOR
BY Victor J. Evans
ATTORNEY

138—Periale siblings. L-R: Ernie Periale Gillia, John Angelo Periale and Margaret Periale D'Ippolito, McGraw Avenue, Bronx, New York, c. 1940.

139—On the Hudson River Dayline, c. 1923. Top, L-R: John Angelo Periale with John Massimo Periale on his lap, Margaret Periale D'Ippolito, Gertrude, Dr. Daoud "David" Himadi with Lily Coda on his lap, Rose Periale Coda with David Himadi on her lap. Bottom: L-R: Albert D'Ippolito, Margaret Periale D'Ippolito, Gertrude with John Massimo Periale on her lap, Dr. Daoud "David" Himadi with David Himadi on his lap, Rose Periale Coda with Lily Coda on her lap.

How Della Periale and Dr. Himadi met: Paolina Cerchio Periale's father Secundo "Parin" Cerchio [Della Periale's maternal grandfather] owned a tavern near Lodi. One of the services provided by the tavern was a stagecoach line. The stagecoach took people to the train line that ran to the ferry that ran to New York City. A lot of local businessmen frequented the tavern. One of them was Dr. Daoud "David" Himadi.

141—Above: Periales and D'Ippolitos, c. 1935. Back row: John Massimo Periale, John Angelo Periale, Albert D'Ippolito. Middle row: Joseph Francis Periale, Paula Periale, Johanna D'Ippolito. Front row: James Gabriel Periale, Joe D'Ippolito. Below: Gertrude and Elizabeth Anne Periale, Spring Lake Heights, New Jersey, c. 1964.

142—Above: Massimo Periale and Paola Cerchio Periale [?]. Below: Massimo Periale [?].

145—Schematic for John Angelo Periale's patented "Periometer," November 6, 1928.

Opposite: Gertrude D'Ippolito in Paterson, New Jersey, c. 1920.

Made in the USA
Middletown, DE
11 October 2023

40568309R00084